T0193621

SPIRITUAL POWER IN
Motion

Ned Byron Pendergast
and Lynne Pendergast Ferdon

WESTBOW
PRESS®
A DIVISION OF THOMAS NELSON
& ZONDERVAN

WestBow Press books may be ordered through booksellers or by contacting:

WestBow Press
A Division of Thomas Nelson & Zondervan
1663 Liberty Drive
Bloomington, IN 47403
www.westbowpress.com
1 (866) 928-1240

ISBN: 978-1-9736-1561-3 (sc)
ISBN: 978-1-9736-1562-0 (hc)
ISBN: 978-1-9736-1560-6 (e)

Library of Congress Control Number: 2018900823

Print information available on the last page.

WestBow Press rev. date: 01/23/2018

We dedicate this book to our father, Norbert Richard Pendergast, who has been an inspiration to us during this lifetime. Our dad was a true gardener who loved the soil, and our Lord God was his guiding light.

> I am the true vine and my Father is the gardener. He cuts off every branch in me that bears no fruit, while every branch that does bear fruit he prunes so that it will be even more fruitful. (John 15:1 NIV)

Cover Acknowledgment

Cover picture by Wendy Pendergast Fendrick

$\mathcal{C}$ontents

Heaven

Light

Miscellaneous

Introduction

Our goal in writing this book is to allow you to read our writings and poems with an open mind and then find your own interpretation. This is why a written journal is so important for when you read your own words later; you will see great changes in your thought process.

We all have to find our own best method to absorb new thoughts that lie dormant within our inner self. My method is early morning meditation upon rising, while for others it may work better at bedtime. The trick to reading *Spiritual Power in Motion* is not to speed read; read just a few pages at a time. Think about what you have read, and then let it go. I like to give it until the next morning and read the same pages. To my amazement, a totally new concept often comes forth. The reason for this is that we live in the present, yet our understanding comes from our past experiences, so we have the benefit of past lessons, and our path to enlightenment moves forward.

Let me give an example. Each morning, you drive down the same country road to work. Today the sun is shining and the leaves on the trees are a deep rich green. Now take this same trip tomorrow, when it is raining with dark clouds and the leaves appear to be a dull green. This is the same drive, but the view is different. It is the same landscape, but you are looking at it in a different light. What I am saying is that all is an illusion, for the only change was in your thinking and what your eyes perceived. Reading follows the same path, so what you are looking for is the true reality. When you allow this concept to happen and you learn this, the worldview will change your life.

The greatest example is the Bible. Read Genesis 1, and then, after a year, read it again, and then read it again in five years. Each time, your understanding will expand via your gains in wisdom and knowledge.

Two thousand years from now, this book will still be relevant. In fact, all spiritual books will be relevant, for the written word doesn't change; it is only the reader's understanding and perception that changes.

So, read slowly and find your own words and thoughts as you read *Spiritual Power in Motion.*

Cause and Effect

Shallow men believe in luck or in circumstances.

Strong men believe in cause & effect.

—Ralph Waldo Emerson
(1803 – 1882)

Cause and Effect

Cause always originates in the subconscious world, or your inner thoughts; it is internal. The effect then only manifests itself in the objective world, or what is called outer self; this is external

What is the true answer to the question of how to control the inner thought process amid the war of negative thoughts that try to cloud the outer thought process? Let's take the example of when Jesus turned the water into wine at the wedding feast. "When the wine was gone, Jesus' mother said to him, 'They have no more wine'" (John 2:3 NIV). Jesus told the servants to fill the jars with water; this was the cause, or the inner self. When the bridegroom tasted the drink, it was fine wine; this was the effect—the outer self. There again we can say the inner energy wave produces the outer result.

Not all cause produces a good effect. If you set in motion an unpleasant or unkind energy wave, remember that the effect will also be unpleasant or unkind. Let's say there is an opportunity for promotion at work but there is another person also vying for the job. If you start rumors of an unkind sort or potentially false comments about the opposition, the effect might be that you get the job. But you are dishonest **and** not really deserving of the job. How can you possibly do a good job when you got the position under false pretenses?

Let's use another example to show how this law works. God created a tomato; it is red, round, and sweet, and it has many seeds. This plant is grown in USA, Europe, and South America; tomatoes are all basically the same. Now keep in mind that the seed (cause) is needed to develop into a plant to produce the tomato (effect). Once the seed is put into the soil, watered, and tended to, it will sprout and grow. Remember: nature knows to let the hull to be eaten away by the bacteria, but it does not destroy the tender young seed. The plant grows and matures, flowers, and produces the promised tomato fruit. This is an excellent example of the cause and effect of our universe.

The cause originates in the inner self; this is where it starts, so be certain and be careful that your thoughts and desires are going to produce the effect you are looking for. Remember that good causes always produce good effects, so it is up to you to choose which path you want to take.

Cause and Effect

How many times have you said that when you solve one problem, another seems to take its place? The truth is that you only thought you corrected or solved the problem. Our heavenly Father created us in perfection, and thus these minor events are ours to handle. This is why we were given our Holy Spirit to be our companion and to help us resolve these issues. You must remember that God created you perfect, for he knows nothing but perfection

We do not realize how many times we set in motion a wrong cause, and then the universal law is that there must be an effect. If, as you start down a new path with bad emotions like anger, fear, hate, or unkindness, this cause will certainly have an effect on those around you.

Correction of an error in total is a good thing, for you will then be better off, and those around you will gain from a righteous reflection.

Bad health and financial woes are all the same concept, for with a negative thought and continued thoughts along this line, you add and add to one cause, and that effect becomes overwhelming. You have to ask yourself, "Why would I do this to myself?"

The answer lies within you. Correction is as easy as asking your spirit guide to help you make corrections to self, or ego. Correct the thoughts (cause) and you will also correct the effect. A healthy mind produces a healthy body.

All things are really the same but with a little twist here and there to confuse you; that is ego's role. Your role is to make this journey as simple as possible, and the only way to do this is to ask for help with all the causes you have started. Remember these words from the Bible: "Avenge not yourself, but rather give place unto wrath; for it is written, Vengeance is mine; I will repay, saith the Lord" (Romans 12:19 KJV).

This means it is not yours to try to correct but his to help you along this path.

Start today to rid yourself of all evil cause and effect, and do the following in private. Make a list of all the things you want gone, not only for your benefit but also for the benefit of those you love. If you don't have at least twenty-five, you are fooling yourself. Sit in a quiet place and turn within to create this list, and add to it when a moment or thought comes. If this seems too hard to believe, just look around you; are you here on Earth and breathing and moving? Who do you think is responsible for this?

Cause and Effect

The law of cause and effect is one of the many laws of creation. No cause can go without there being an effect as a result of that cause. This is similar to the law of opposites; there cannot be good without bad, warm without cold, happy without sad, and on and on it goes.

Cause always starts on the inner self, and via the mind it starts in motion an energy wave. This energy wave is not something you can see, as it is internal. This will be the start of creation, or the cause, which in turn will produce an effect.

Effect occurs when you allow this energy wave to pass from the inner self to the outer world. This energy then takes this matter and turns it into something you then can see and touch, or even just feel.

You start with an idea—a cause—and you allow your energy to process this into an effect for all to enjoy. Take the wheel as an example. First comes the thought within the mind that this might be a good invention. Then the building of the wheel takes the mind working with the hands and the energy to produce that round cylinder called the wheel. The cause was the idea of a wheel, and the effect was the actual production of the wheel. The effect is also the joy everyone feels in putting this item to work.

Another example: An artist comes up with an idea for a painting; it is just forming in his mind. He picks up the paintbrush and lets his creative energy take over. The effect is a beautiful artwork for all to see and enjoy. This is true for the doctor, the scientist, schoolteachers, and musicians. They each have a cause, and it produces an effect.

Man cannot take credit for these divine skills and insights, because this is a gift from heaven. This is truly the universal mind at work.

"If you prove the **cause**, you at once prove the **effect**; and conversely nothing can exist without its cause." (Aristotle, *Rhetoric*)

Cause and Effect—Discipline

It was your mother and father who taught you discipline as you grew up, which in turn makes you a better person today. This planet has many sets of laws, or disciplines, to be followed. When you break these laws, the universal law we all know comes into play, which is the law of cause and effect. Of course, we don't know many of these laws on the conscious level, but they are still there. This is why events happen over and over again in different ways until we understand them and learn right from wrong.

Some disciplines are not pretty and are downright painful, yet we learn and many times look back and say, "It was a good thing." How many times when bad things come your way do you say it is bad karma from another lifetime or another situation? I say most likely you are wrong, for cause and effect happen at the same time; they are a chain reaction happening one after the other. You must accept the responsibility of your actions and be careful of what cause and effect you put into play.

The Holy Spirit has all the wisdom … trust it; let it be your guide!

Unfoldment

The true law of the universe is to let everything unfold in its own time. But we, as self or humans, like to inject our thoughts and wishes, which can confuse these laws.

What I am saying here is to curb your mind and let the spiritual side of you work to unfold your desires. This is a major switch in most of us, for we are always injecting our own thoughts and the actions we want to occur. Why? Because we have been taught that and think nothing will change in our lives unless we take action and promote it.

The unseen world of the Holy Spirit knows everything, so believe that less is better than more. Cause, however, starts from within, so make your thoughts brief and to the point. Leave it to your spirit guide to determine how the effect will appear. Your job, then, when your wish unfolds, is to follow as directed. Remember: words can sometimes have various meanings, so be careful what you ask for.

Here is an example of how thoughts put into words may not be what is wanted. A person who has worked for fifty years and says out loud, "I want to retire and do nothing." Behold, that person ends up in a retirement home, sick, weak, bored, and lonely. Now, if he had asked in a different way and said, "I want to retire happy," he would be on vacation, playing golf, and tending his garden, happy as can be.

So, the lesson here is that if you ask, you will receive; but be sure you are asking for the correct thing. Then let it unfold, and you will see how your thoughts and prayers are answered.

Cause and Effect

Sit quietly and ponder your plans for this event.
Your thoughts must portray what you truly meant.
Your cause must be true and have a goal to be made.
Your decision is the effect so that others may be swayed.
The cause will put in motion waves of energy and power.
The effect will be a result of all this energy to empower.
Think wisely, for all cause has an important effect.
Universal mind will guide you to keep everything in check.

Cause Always Results in an Effect

A cause always starts with the inner self's thought.
Like a chain reaction, an effect is sought.
Take the artist who draws pictures as he is led,
The musician who composes songs in his head.
First is the cause, then the effect comes into view.
This reaction is felt or seen as a creation within you.
Man cannot take credit for this marvelous skill.
The cause and effect are beyond our own will.
Our lives are guided by our heavenly Father from above.
Be humble; be grateful for the guidance we do love.

Emotion

The best and most beautiful things in
the world cannot be seen or even touched.

They must be felt with the heart.

—Helen Keller (1880–1968)

Faith

"According to your faith let it be done to you" (Matthew 9:29 NIV). To get your positive thinking going, you have to believe. It would help to focus on yourself for a change, maybe centering on your health, family, or something personal. The reason I use the word "self" is that it will work on anything, but if other souls are involved, you may think it just happened by accident or by luck and not through faith.

To start, you have to stop thinking in opposites. One cannot have faith if one is thinking in the negative. Faith is a positive attitude between you and the Creator. Think about it; when you start to pray, is it the outside world you see, which is made up of matter, or is it the spiritual concept, which is made up of the Holy Spirit? The answer is that it should be only the spiritual concept.

The great thing about the spiritual world is that it has no favorites. Everyone is equal there. Another great point is that it also has no concept of time, meaning that by faith or, if you prefer, by prayer, you can receive it today, tomorrow, or immediately.

One must have a positive attitude about faith. We are all created in perfection; we must therefore believe this with our whole heart. Is it any wonder that this attitude will improve every facet of your life!

This world has what I call an intelligent concept of laws. Everything good is just waiting for you to ask for it. But keep in mind that in order to receive, you must first make the request. Just thinking it is as good as a verbal request. But remember: the bad news is that if you are feeling negative and your request is not answered, then you should not be surprised that your request has fallen on deaf ears. Faith is believing with your whole heart that your prayers and requests will be answered in good time.

Jesus said to the centurion, "Go! It will be done just as you believe it would" (Matthew 8:13 NIV). And his servant was healed at that very hour. Believing is another form of faith. By faith you can be led out of the darkness and into the light. By faith you gain a new vision to see your life as it can be. New horizons will open up before you, and you can experience the pathway that God intended you to travel.

Faith to Heal

Let's start with two quotes from Jesus Christ

1. "Ask, and it shall be given you; seek, and ye shall find; knock, and it shall be opened unto you." (Matthew 7:7–8 KJV)
2. "Go! Let it be done just as you believed it would." (Matthew 8:13 KJV)

We all know that while Jesus walked the earth, he healed hundreds of people. Yet as time passed and Christ was raised back to the Father in heaven, these healings were not said to be "faith healings" but rather miracles. This concept was wrong. Faith is the strong belief in reality, not in miracles. In reality, all creation was perfect. Jesus Christ showed this to us time and time again. When Christ healed, it was nothing more than bringing the truth to the forefront. Man was created perfect, and Jesus was bringing mankind back to that state through divine faith.

Our role, then, is to have faith to know that all was created perfect; this then covers all facets of our life. You can start to improve your faith by doing the following: Take a notepad and write all the good things that have happened in your lifetime. When you look at the list, thank our heavenly Father for these blessings. Remember: ask, and it shall be given you. Your faith in the Lord has made all things possible.

Forget all the perceived bad things, for they are not important at this juncture. But keep in mind that what may have seemed a truly bad thing in the end turned into a truly good thing, for it helped you to grow. An example is that if you burn your hand on the stove, you thereafter are more careful and have a respect for fire. If you crash your car because you are texting, yes it is a bad thing, but perhaps you get a ticket, pay a fine, and have to make major repairs to your car. Lesson learned: do not text and drive.

Faith will solve every issue in your life, but it will not necessarily do so next week or even next month. The Lord God knows when it is the right time to resolve your issues and send his blessing to you.

God gave us free thought for a reason; it is our biggest gift. When asking for a solution to a problem, never state how you think the problem should be resolved, for that is the job of the Holy Spirit—to guide you to a correct conclusion. We must correct our thoughts, have true faith, and trust in the Lord; then all things are possible.

Faith

Having faith is nothing more than a strong belief via your mind.
Thought forms then enters the ether and heads upward to the divine.
Christ taught us this during his stay here on Earth,
Giving us confidence as we moved along with each rebirth.
To quote, "It is done unto you as you believe."
As one believes, so our faith is renewed and glory retrieved
To regain your belief in faith, write all the positive in your life.
You will then see that you had many of life's problems right.
Faith is bringing reality back to this Earth plane.
Faith is through prayer, as we have so much to gain.

Fear

Fear is an emotion that we overcome every day without even being aware of it. As we drive to work, we have full confidence that we will get there in one piece. Yet in the back of our minds, we know we must be vigilant, drive within the speed limit, look before changing lanes, stop at intersections, and observe all the good rules of driving. If we let fear control the way we drive, we would spend more time trying to decide whether or not a maneuver was a correct one and perhaps cause an accident because of our hesitation.

Fear takes many forms in our everyday life, and if one is not careful, it will control one's life. There is the fear of leaving one's home, fear of heights, fear of being robbed, and on and on goes the list. Fear puts you in that negative realm, and therefore negative things will occur.

Fear should have no power over you, because fear is the negative thoughts running around in your mind. Fear creeps in if you leave the door open and let the dark thought in. Remember: your spirit guide is your guiding light and will lead you out of darkness and thus help you destroy your fears.

Do not fear what happened yesterday, for that is gone and you cannot change it. Do not fear the future, because your fear just might make that happen. Live today in the present, and with the help of our Creator, get control over your fear, face the devil, and come out on the winning side into the light.

Let me point something out that is so simple you will wonder why you didn't see this before. The power to create comes from the light; fear is powerless if there is light. The difference is that in the light you can see things that you and others have created; you can see trees, buildings, and all that exists on Earth. Now tell me what you can see in the darkness. You can see nothing there, because darkness has no power; fear is in darkness.

The next time fear starts to creep into your thoughts, just think, "FEAR—false evidence appearing real."

Happiness

The definition of happiness is a mental or emotional state of well-being defined by positive or pleasant emotions ranging from contentment to intense joy. Okay, that gives us something to think about. Happiness is a mental or emotional state. If you are feeling positive and life looks really good, then you are in a happy place.

It is very important to remember that your happiness come directly from within yourself. Other people are not responsible for making you a happy person. Again, we see the law of opposites come into play. If you are a happy individual, then all those who come in contact with you will also express happiness. Yet if you are burdened with negative thoughts and actions, then you are responsible for your own unhappiness, and you even cause unhappiness to others. "A happy heart makes the face cheerful, but heartache crushes the spirit" (Proverbs 15:13 NIV).

Happiness is a frame of your mind, not that of others. Never depend on a spouse, sibling, friend, or coworker for your own happiness, as this is your responsibility. The more you do in God's kingdom, the happier you will be. Being involved in church, school, volunteerism, and even work can bring happiness to your life. The one who sits home and says, "What about me?" is going to be lonely and sad because that person's energy is centered on self and not on those around him or her.

On a more spiritual side, happiness can be found while walking in the woods, skiing on a mountaintop, or sitting quietly and looking at the ocean. Those quiet times alone with nature bring you closer to our heavenly Father, and we learn to appreciate all that he has created. "This is the day the LORD has made; let us rejoice and be glad in it" (Psalm 118:24 NIV).

Happiness

Never depend on your happiness to come from others.
While an infant, happiness is given by love of a mother.
As you mature, you must look inward, for happiness is self.
Remember to express it and not keep it bottled on the shelf.
We generate and exude this marvelous emotion.
Those around us will benefit from this powerful potion.
It's not to be taken lightly, for it's a gift to behold.
Happiness will make our life so good until we are old.
Others may say happiness comes with great wealth.
Remember it's not true; happiness comes from self.
Happiness is a frame of mind, so be joyous; be glad.
People pick up on our emotions, so do not pass on sad.
Open your heart and let the rays shine through.
It's a wondrous day, so let's all express happiness anew.

Be Strong, Be Happy

It is easy to be happy when life flows right along.
A soul's real worth comes when one can smile when things go wrong.
Our best test comes by correcting trouble year after year,
For true passion comes when we are able to smile through the tears.
I want a life that is filled with happiness and joy
That chaos and violence around me cannot destroy.
Try to see only the goodness and joy; you then will be happy and glad.
Wonder of wonders, for soon you will forget that you ever were sad.

—Author unknown, similar to Ella Wilcox circa 1906

Joy

What a powerful emotion joy is. It is happiness, contentment, and peace of mind all rolled into one. We all have known people who express joy, and these are the people we want to spend our time with. Joyful people make you happy just by being around them; they lift your spirits.

Joy is something from within self. You cannot acquire joy or say, "I wish I had joy." It is something deep within our soul that expresses itself like a shining light bubbling to the surface. A person who is happy and very content with his or her life will automatically express joy.

The one thing to be very careful of is not to steal someone else's joy. An individual who has a negative outlook on life can easily, by unkind comments or actions, rob a joyful person who is a positive thinker.

The spiritual side of joy is mentioned many times in the Bible. It is the state of the heart and the soul residing in each of us. When we have the joy of the Lord God, we know it, and so do those around us, for we cannot help but express this joy. As stated in Romans 15:13 (KJV), "Now the God of hope fill you with all joy and peace in believing, that you may abound in hope, through the power of the Holy Ghost."

Joy Is a Special Gift

Joy is a special gift sent from above.
God gave us this wondrous gift of love.
Our joy has so many different stages.
The gambit of feeling within us rages.
From pleasure to delight to peace and more,
The emotions of joy start in our very core.
Spiritual joy is the state of the heart.
Believe, for that is where it all starts.
Joy is our very inner soul to express.
Spread the Joy so that all you can bless.

Love

Do you ever sit quietly and think about all the different types of love there are?

- love of others, parents, spouses, children, and even dearest friends
- love of nature and all the beauty it provides
- love of activities like baseball, skiing, running, gardening, and writing
- love of home, where you find peace and contentment
- love of God, the center of your very being

This list could go on and on, reaching out to every facet of your life. When you experience each of these loves, it gives you great happiness and joy. A person who has love in his or her life will reap the benefits of this wonderful emotion.

In the material world, love can have multiple phases for both good and bad. If your love and drive is to strive to have many worldly possessions, such as money, success, and things, you have missed the boat, because you cannot take any of this stuff with you to the heavenly world. But if you use this wealth to share with those in need and do not make this wealth a power only you can enjoy, then you have truly accomplished the true meaning of love.

Love of self can also be another of the "bad" emotions of love. Individuals who are so self-centered that they only think of what is best for them cannot experience the joy and happiness of sharing and caring for others.

A child knows love from the minute of conception. The mother rubs her belly in a loving caress, and the child senses this. A child will recognize the sound of the mother's voice and be soothed. This child will be born and knows immediately that it is loved even though he or she is too young to verbalize the emotion.

In the spiritual world, love is the strongest of all emotions. "For God so loved the world, that he gave his one and only Son, that whoever believes in him should not perish but have eternal life" (John 3:16 NIV). How many stories in the Bible tell of the great love and faith in God his children have displayed? Abraham was willing to sacrifice his only son, Isaac, in order to obey the Word of God. That was certainly true love and faith in the Lord.

Jesus Christ continually expressed his love of his disciples and all people in the many miracles he performed. His greatest love was for his heavenly Father. When he was crucified, he knew this was the path his Father had set out for him; that was the purest form of love.

It is important that we know that "love is something we do, not just something to say." It can be so easy to say "I love you," but remember that this means you must be a caring, kindly person and physically show this by the things you do to make a person happy, safe, and content. The old saying "Actions speak louder than words" is a good thing to keep in mind.

Let me share an experience I had over twenty years ago. Each morning, I spend time in meditation and connecting with my spirit guide. This particular morning, I regressed back to a past life. This is why I believe in rebirth, as each stage is a stepping stone to the time you ascend to the heavenly world. I was a shepherd boy of twelve. As I tended my sheep, I saw a cloud of dust coming from the road to Galilee with one hundred people following the Lord Jesus Christ. I was on the top of a rocky mountain about a mile away, and I ran down this rocky slope but got only a quarter of a mile from the road as Christ passed. At that moment, he saw me and waved.

As I was just writing this, my eyes filled with tears and I was overcome with a feeling of bliss. The atmosphere around me changed, and that same feeling of peace and love passed through me.

Below are some Bible passages that express the true meaning of love.

> My command is this: Love each other as I have loved you. Greater love has no one than this, that he lay down his life for his friends. (John 15:12–13 NIV)

> Love is patient, love is kind. It does not envy, it does not boast, it is not proud. It is not rude, it is not self-seeking, it is not easily angered, it keeps no record of wrongs. Love does not delight in evil but rejoices with the truth. It always protects, always trusts, always hopes, always perseveres. Love never fails … (1 Corinthians 12:4–8 NIV)

> "Love the Lord your God with all your heart and with all your soul and with all your mind and with all your strength. The second is this: You shall love your neighbor as yourself. There is no other commandment greater than these." (Mark 12:30–31 NIV)

Art of Love

I ponder, is love an act of thought,
Or is it something that is taught?
We have five senses; maybe they are the trigger for the picture of love.
Or maybe it is nothing more than an energy force from above.
Wherever it comes from, it is not only a human function,
For observe animals' behavior and you will see love in action.
Sometimes I view wildlife so fancy and free.
I pray to Spirit that it will continue with me.
Love here on earth has a far different meaning than above,
For in the heavenly worlds, we are all one, so it is natural and easy to love.
Some may feel that to be one, we give up our personal thoughts.
Yet this is wrong, for we gain the power which we have always sought.
The power of the collective for the purpose of perfection is bliss.
This is the heavenly Father's gift to us all with a hug and a kiss.
Love is always in motion and has no borders.
It is meant to be shared and never hoarded.
The power of love is never demonic.
Rather its nature is for good and travels through space supersonic.
Yes, love is the act of thought!
Yes, love is something we are all taught.

Love Is Something We Do

Have you ever wondered about the emotion of love?
Do you think it starts here on Earth or from above?
As a young child, you might love your cuddly stuffed toy.
As an adult, you love the happiness and everlasting joy.
Love is something we do, not something we say.
Love is the quiet time we spend each day to pray.
How easy to say the word "love" and let it pour forth.
Is it just another word in the vocabulary to show our worth?
The best love is the kind that awakens the soul.
Express love by actions, and your life will surely unfold.
Action is loving thy neighbor as you would love yourself.
Love expressed to all will in turn be returned to your own self.

Valentine's Day, 1942

Darling,

It seems like a good kind of day to tell you how much I love you. Of course, it would be impossible to tell you how much, but maybe I can give you an inkling.

It seems strange to me, but when I married you, I knew I loved you. After we were married a year, I knew I loved you more. So it went each year. I was conscious of loving you so much more, adoring you so much more, respecting you so much more.

This past year I have been so conscious of a great admiration for you. I do so admire your kindness, your generosity, your tolerance, your courage, and, of course, your great sense of honesty.

It seems like after living with you for over twelve years, I might know you inside out or, as some say, like a book. Instead I am continually discovering more and more of you, not replacing the dear you I know but continually adding to you. Probably this all accounts for my loving you more and more all the time. I am constantly finding more of you to love, and love added to love equals more love.

So, in sum total, I do love you very dearly—more than I can ever tell you. And so you will understand that I don't tell you how much I love you because there is no measurement by which to measure it. But maybe on top of all this, I can inveigle you to let me be your valentine.

Guess who?

> Written by Gladys C. Pendergast to her husband, Norbert Richard Pendergast Jr., in 1942. Tradition held that on Valentine's Day, one never signed one's name—keep them guessing!

Note: "Inveigle" means "To win over by coaxing, flattery, or artful talk." When I saw this word, I did not know it, but I knew Mother was a very good speller,

so I looked it up on the internet.

Healing

This is what the Lord, the God of your
father David, says: I have heard your
prayer and seen your tears. I will heal you.

—2 Kings 20:5 (NIV)

Concept of Healing

How does one (self) go about healing oneself? Healing can take many forms: an illness, a business issue, family estrangement, and many others. The power of the mind to heal or correct misconceptions of healing is nothing more than the correction of your thinking. This means not allowing temptation or evil to creep into your mind and present evil ungodly thoughts. In order to heal yourself, you must change your thinking to allow only pure and spiritual thoughts to enter your mind. For example, if you are under a lot of stress, you might feel as though you have the beginning of a headache. But you can correct your thinking and say, "Yes, I am under a great deal of stress, but I will work through it with the help of my spirit guide." Change you thinking and dwell on the positive, and do not give the negative feelings the power to control your well-being.

To heal any disease or difficult situation, one has to know that it came from either the inner self or the outer self, but it always had to first come from the mind. There is no doubt about this, for the body has no power to create; it is the mind that has this power.

Healing works by the power of the mind because we are one. My mind and yours together can get the wheel of correction in motion. Let's say you have a toothache. You go to the dentist, and he tells you he can help you. He drills the decayed spot in your tooth, fills it, and off you go. He, the doctor, was the practitioner or healer. He set his mind and yours on the same track, and behold, pain is gone. Always remember that the Lord Jesus healed in an instant through faith and true belief that he and our Lord God could perform miracles as one. For us it may take a little longer, but we must also have faith and truly believe; then this miracle will happen.

One should remember that disease takes time to mature; therefore, focus on perfect ideas of the self and body. Healing, as I have said before, is done on the subconscious or inner thoughts, for as creation moves to the objective, or outer, thoughts, it has to follow what the inner mind created. In other words, mind over matter. The inner self, the mind, does have control over the outer self, which is the essence of matter.

Healing Disease

I truly do not like this subject, for I don't want to give it power. Yet one may ask oneself, "How could I have a problem with my health that I have never even heard of or thought about?" We have only one creative mind, and that is what we call the universal mind, which is controlled by the universal laws. These laws have no idea what is large or small, rich or poor, or even black or white. These are left to the objective mind (the outer external self) and the subjective mind (inner thoughts). I, myself, would call them conscious and subconscious thoughts. They have intelligence, but they do not have the power to create. Creation comes from the self's universal mind. This is where free thought is in control.

Back to the idea of how one could have a problem in health without one's knowledge beforehand. This is simple. Remember: laws know not of good or bad. You or your inner "Self" become aware and then make that choice. Say you are walking to your garden to plant tomato seeds. On your way, unknown to you, a few seeds drop from your hand. You get to the garden and plant the seeds. You water and tend to your garden. One week later, you have germination and a row of tomatoes. Now, would not the seed you dropped have germinated as well? Yes, of course, but you were not in control of the germination process. It was Mother Nature who had a hand in this miracle. This is another example of the laws of the universe taking control.

What I am trying to say here is that you have to be aware of what comes into your space. By "space" I mean your conscious thinking. If it is a test of disease, you have to correct your thinking right away. Your thoughts have to acknowledge that the laws of our universe do not know the difference between good or evil. So, it is you who has to confirm this conception. The body was created perfect in every way, but it only has power generated by the mind to correct error and move forward to perfection.

Healing the Body

This writing took more than four days to work out. Looking back, I wonder why this true revelation took so long. The reason is that the life we see here on Earth clouds our judgment. How can you not think that what we see during this lifetime is nothing more than an illusion by the smart master, Ego? Our universal mind is the healer. For it is the creator of reality. The heavenly mind created the body. The ego cannot create; it can only give us illusion. I used to say to myself that the ego always gives us something and then creates something bad to take it away. This is wrong, for the ego can create nothing. It is our own power of creation that can create good. For example, the human body is perfect. See its complexity; only the ego can fool us into thinking otherwise.

We drop our guard. A business is created perfect, just the same as your car. What changes? We allow the evil ego to step in and corrupt everything. Have a relationship? Keep the ego out. To heal the body, you must first heal the mind. The body remains the guilty messenger. Guilt, like sin, holds us in chains, for both are nothing more than an error in want of correction. We have all the tools to rid ourselves of the hold of the ego. We are the Creator! We have the power to rid ourselves of illusions and let the Holy Spirit prevail. Allow your higher self to guide you every day.

I know what I am talking about. Two weeks ago, via the Holy Spirit, I changed my thinking about my wife of fifty-five years. I see her differently. We both have changed. Love has returned. I see and hear it from her mouth and actions. We talk and laugh together. This is only the start. The illusion of old age is gone. We are a couple again. It was like my wife was lost, and now we are taking back control of our own creation.

Grace is letting go of error, guilt, and fear, and allowing our higher self, our spirit, to take back control. The real Source, the heavenly Father, created us to be happy. The ego's role is to help us to become strong and see the power we have to create perfection.

Mind is that powerful energy outside our body, and it is just waiting for our correction to achieve perfection. Praise the Lord!

Healing Is Our Power

What self is trying to build here on earth is the knowledge and acceptance that mankind has the power to do anything. Christ showed us this awesome power.

We are not ready yet to perform these miracles, as at this point we do not have the faith. We need to acknowledge and accept the fact as written in Genesis, chapter 1, which states that God gave man "dominion over all things." God made man in his image and likeness, which is perfect.

Say you cut your finger and you think it will be healed in seven days, and behold, in seven days it is healed. Why did this happen? Because you believed it would happen. The fact is, it could have been healed in a second if you truly believed.

Say you go to the doctor and he gives you pills to last seven days to correct an illness. What happens? You feel better because you believed the time frame the doctor gave you.

The truth is—and this is okay—we are just not ready to acknowledge our true power. Through prayer and closeness to our heavenly Father, we, too, will be able to perform miracles just as his Son, Jesus Christ, did.

No Man Walks Life's Road Alone (Al-One)

As of September 5, 2012, my goal for the next thirty days was to become a practitioner of healing. As a self-healer, I have been great over the years; yet as life moves on, the evil ego steps in so that you lose faith. I asked my mom years ago if I ever was sick in school. From age five to age eighteen, never; while in the Marines, never; from age twenty-one to age seventy-four, maybe ten times at most. I will, via my inner spirit, disclose the reason for this.

My goal, however, is not to heal myself, but to heal others, including those I will never see or know. I want to share my good fortune with all, via the Holy Spirit.

Let's get started. Say a friend comes to me unwell. He tells me everything, and as a friend I listen to him ramble. That is my first mistake, for I am enforcing the sickness. My attention while he discusses the facts should be to know that "he is the perfect image and likeness of God."

There are laws in play here on Earth. We all know of cause and effect via the power of thought, so our first step is to know. My friend needs correction of mind, and the correction comes via a strong belief in myself to complete this task. I am "the perfect image and likeness of God." That's the start. The universe is just waiting for our command.

What I need to do is know that I have for years done this for myself and believe I can do it for others. Spirit just last night—September 6, 2012—told me this is a twenty-four-hour job for thirty days. With the power of free thought, you can never allow a second of negative thought to slip in.

Prayers Heard

Every time I feel I have moved ahead in my spiritual growth, I get a wake-up call to my inner self. We learn in steps in this spiritual growth, one step at a time, and we cannot rush or forge ahead too quickly.

From a nonspiritual side, we are different in color, accent, religion, and even the name we are called. But from a spiritual point of view, we are all the same. We are all one; we are all children of God. We were each born in God's image and likeness—perfection in all.

Praying for results has to be directed not toward self but to all, for we are one. That which benefits self will benefit all. For example, if you want to bless a loved one in need, ask to bless all that are in need. Secondly, never limit your prayers to just one thing, for Christ and the Holy Spirit know what is good for everyone.

Pray to reduce poverty, to heal the sick in body and mind, and to protect the little children. It is impossible for an honest prayer of goodwill not to be answered. Yet it is possible that you may not know it was answered. God always answers our prayers, but it will be in his time, not in ours here on Earth. God knows when it is time to answer the prayer with healing results.

The Body

To be quite honest, I don't think I have been giving the body its due respect. I have said many times it is like a piece of clay and has no power on its own, and that it is no different than a log left lying on the ground. But I have to admit I was so wrong.

First, the body is like all living things. It is a miracle in its complexity. True, it takes orders via the conscious mind within, but it has no control of the subconscious mind. The truth is that the body is the product of what the inner self believes. So the body was created as the perfect image and likeness, for its pure perfection is and always will be. It is not the body's fault when it is not perfect. It is you and I that have the power to correct our inner thoughts. The body acts only on what our conscious mind tells it to do.

The body is our best friend; we need to perfect our mind's thoughts. When something turns up on the body that is not perfect, we need to correct our conscious inner thought immediately. Remember: this holds true for the outer material world as well. The subjective world of the unconscious mind has to follow the world of creations. These inner thought forms are the start of creation that we see daily. It is just as easy to create positive thoughts as it is to create negative ones.

If you look around, you will see millions more positive thoughts and actions as compared to the negative, so we are doing well with the tools of free thought that God has given us, and, of course, with our ever-present spirit guides.

We each choose our own way to correct negative thoughts, but what we all have in common is a strong belief in perfection. And via help from our maker, mind correction is possible. Reading another person's words is okay, but we each have to find our own words, so just sit quiet and make yourself ready to listen.

Universe of Healing

Conscious mind works in the inner self, or the objective world. The unconscious mind works in the outer self, or the subjective world. The power of creation comes from both of these forms; the inner self and the outer self work together to achieve a given goal. But the subjective world, or the outer self, can never reject objective creation. This is the law of the universe!

Let's use the body as an example. You are in control of this body form 100 percent of the time. You control what it thinks, what it does, and how it acts, and this list goes on and on. But it is your free will that guides you in all you do. You go to a concert with loud music, and when it is time to go home, you have a splitting headache. This is the conscious mind stating that it is not feeling well. This effect is then transferred to the subjective you, or the outer self. The mind says you have a headache, and your body reacts to this stimulus or suggestion, and you are left with a whopper of a headache.

This is where universal healing comes into play. Correct your inner thinking so your outer self can also change its effect. We have all known people who have changed their conscious mind via prayer to correct the effect on the outer self.

The addict, the sick, the abused—these can all be turned around by prayer. Prayer turns your thinking around so you are asking the heavenly Father to heal you rather than sitting around feeling oh, so sorry for yourself.

If your body is feeling sick, it needs correction from within; sickness shows on the outer self because the subjective world can never reject the inner creation. So healing comes from the belief within. The same holds true of thought forms to start and grow a business, build a house, or raise a child. Everything starts from the inner world via your spirit and prayer.

Your body follows your thoughts and creates an event or effect. It is your Free Will that is the cause and effect of your world. The good part about this is that everything you see, feel, or touch, as well as events, came first from within you. Want change? Believe in self-creation. Strong thoughts create a strong path on the outer self to achieve higher goals.

I know that for me personally, reading sparks my mind to think, but my own words come from within, so the light comes on every morning for me. Each and every one of us has to find his or her own path. I write what I am told in my daily meeting with my spirit guide.

Blessing

It is universal that when sneezing people say, "God bless,"
It's given for the wrong reason, so I'll clear up this mess.
It has nothing to do with your health or getting a cold;
This is a myth that we all have been told.
The truth of the matter is, sneezing is a negative force.
All the evil inside wants to take a positive course.
When totally healthy, I take in a deep breath and sneeze.
This exhalation relieves all negative thoughts in a breeze.
"God bless you" allows all the positive thoughts in.
This removed an evil thought that many call sin.

Prayer Includes All

Because I know self as one, I therefore have love for all others.
I see that God's plan is not separation but to love all our brothers.
Being in this world of chaos, it is important we all band together as one.
What was chaos was a false perception, for God created this world for fun.
When you pray to bless a loved one, include all other souls as well.
The power to correct your thoughts will remove that hard-core shell
Pray only for the better outcome, for Spirit knows best
The prayer is answered in an instant, so knowing this, you can rest.

The Road to Healing

The truth is, the body has no power except via our mind.
Let your guard down and the negative forces aren't too kind.
The body, like your car, has no power until you take control.
Insert the key, start the car, and you can then go on patrol.
Taking back control is nothing more than mind over matter.
So what appears from above always makes decisions better.
Sickness is nothing more than a wrong perception to the right,
For creation is perfect; let your thoughts flow with healing in sight.
Need guidance? Your Spirit is always available for help.
In that moment, self will know the corrections to be felt.
The healing is pure, your control is intact, and your faith is strong.
All is well, and sickness gone; you will be exactly where you belong.

Heaven

He had a dream in which he saw a stairway
resting on the earth, with its top reaching to
heaven, and the angels of God were
ascending and descending on it.

—Genesis 28:12 (NIV)

Heavenly Father

Let's start with a profound fact right off the bat; then I will try to make it clear with as few words as possible. Without the belief of billions of souls, the title above could not exist.

Look at the days when Rome ruled 80 percent of the population. It was not pretty. Men killed one another for sport to please crowds of thousands, first with lions and then the cross. Today these games are gone because mankind took no interest in them. But let's look also at modern-day sports. I love football, yet let's say in time there comes to be not one soul interested in this event anymore; it is then gone.

What this means is the following: "And God said, Let us make man in our image, after our likeness: and let them have dominion over the fish of the sea, and over the fowl of the air, and over the cattle, and over all the earth ..." (Genesis 1:26 KJV). The focus of mind or spirit in masse creates energy via a strong vibration, along with the collective perception; and behold: creation. This comes via the light, which then creates forms. This is the reason, and it is confirmed by science that everything is nonmatter, for with this concept things that have form can change at will via the collective thought process. We as humans have no clue the power we have. We are one, which means that if the Lord Jesus was able to heal the sick or rise from the dead, then we, if we believe, can do the same thing.

You will note that for thirty years I have always asked Spirit to give me earthly examples, for as the Lord's Prayer states, "Thy kingdom come Thy will be done in earth, as it is in heaven" (Mark 6:10 KJV). I would guess that 90 percent of the people today believe that via evolution or Adam and Eve came the birth of the human form. This is not true, for the body is nothing but a tool used in time and space and has no power whatsoever. It is the Holy Spirit, via our free will, that controls the body.

Creation is not enacted by a single entity; creation is enacted by the power of the collective. We are one, which means we were, some thirteen billion years ago, a part of creation. You need to think this through and think outside the box rather than relying on the body's eyes or the feelings, which are restricted by a closed mind. You have experienced the power of many several times, for when a mass of people all think the same way, it has power. Take, for instance, when you are in church and all focus on love, or when you are at a sporting event and our national anthem is sung. It is a fact that in sports, home field advantage is not a myth; the power of oneness causes the home team to play better, allowing them to win more than 80 percent of the time.

Another word I might use is "evolution." This planet's role was created thirteen billion years ago, before there ever was a human to walk the planet. When our time on Earth is gone, it will not be because we did something bad, but because we completed our role here and it is time for a new experience.

So when we pray to our heavenly Father, we are praying to the power of the collective, or self. You should also note that all prayers are answered, yet you may not be ready for the results when they arrive. As an example, how many times has something happened that seemed really bad and changed your life, and then, some time later, you look back and say to yourself, "That was the best thing that happened to me, and it changed my life."

Look around you; all that you see are things that we as humans have created via our free will and thought process. To create the typewriter, someone created the thought of a typewriter and put it into action. Everything is created when the time is right, and not before then. For example, the horse-drawn carriage was put aside and gave way to the auto; this had to wait for gas to be invented. The airplane had to wait till high-powered gas was refined, and this goes on and on.

With new thoughts and new inventions come problems to be solved; this is how we grow and gain knowledge and wisdom. In this manner, we learn development, which leads to perfection. This world you and I invented is multifaceted and is not just what you see in this vibration of time in this year; this planet is more complex, like a movie theater complex that has many different movies all playing at one time. We may be in one theater, but we are unable to see what is going on in the other shows. Take the movie example again: you go to the theater to see a movie, you sit in a chair, you watch a show, you cry or laugh, and the movie ends. You get up from your seat and leave. What happens next is that another person comes in and sits in your same seat and the cycle repeats itself again. This whole concept is important, for I am trying to show you that we are not controlled by other people or events; we have free will, meaning that we are the controllers of our microcosms. You create your todays.

If you were to really examine this world we live in, you would see and feel that it is not just humans that know. Everything you see knows; it is only humans that are aware that they know. It is important to know that everything you see is made up of light, as light is Spirit in different forms. Here is an example: You are standing at a lake's edge. You look across this lake, and about two miles away you see a person pitching a large tent. With a hammer, he is putting in metal stakes at each corner. You see him hit a stake with the hammer, and a few seconds later, you hear the noise. Light travels at 186,000 miles per second, while sound travels at only 740 miles per second. This tells you that what you see with your eyes is always light.

Back to the topic of knowing, if you put a seed in the ground, the seed knows what it is. Of course, it does not know in the same way a human would think. The seed, if put in dry soil, will stay dormant. Add water and the bacteria in the soil will eat the protective dead covering, and only then will the seed germinate. Tell me, how do the bacteria know to stop and not eat the soft tissue of the seed? This seed then will do its job and bear fruit and more seeds so the cycle can start repeating itself, much the same as human rebirth. We witness all these miracles and never give them a second thought.

Thoughts of Heaven

Heaven is not a place where there are buses, cars, trains, and people walking around in beautiful designer clothes. Heaven, for each of us, is our own private interpretation of what that place will be like. By our free thought, we can decide what we would like to believe this holiest of holy places will be like.

Christ Jesus stated, "I and the Father are One" (John 10:30 NIV). Therefore, Jesus as the Son of God ascended to heaven to sit at the right hand of his Father. We are also the children of the loving God, so we shall also ascend to heaven to be with our Father. As children of God, our greatest moment in life comes when we experience the feeling of oneness with our heavenly Father. "So God created man in his own image, in the image of God created he him; male and female created he them" (Genesis 1:27 KJV).

Take the example of Jacob in Genesis 28:16–17 (KJV): "Then Jacob awoken out of his sleep and said, Surely the Lord is in this place, I knew it not. And he was afraid, and said, "How dreadful is this place! this is none other but the house of God, and this is the gate of heaven."

There are many life stories of people who have had near-death experiences and related the wonder of what their eyes saw just before their physical body returned to this planet, Earth. So the conclusion is that to us, heaven is a place in our mind, a place we feel comfortable going to, and a place where we will be reunited with those we love. Heaven is personal and offers the great comfort that we know where we will be going when our time is over.

In Heaven All Are One

The lesson today is the idea that in heaven we are all one.
This idea to some may not feel like it is much fun.
If oneness is true, do we have the ability to choose?
The answer is no, for together in love we can never lose.
Because of the power of light, this world becomes true.
Don't focus on self; embrace oneness for heavenly power.
Oneness is the creation of light upon us like a shower.
All are joyous for eternity, for happiness is near.
There is light at the end of the tunnel, so there is nothing to fear.

Our Father Who Art in Heaven

How many times during the week do we recite the words Jesus Christ gave us from his Sermon on the Mount? This one has special meaning. "Our Father who art in Heaven." (Matthew 6: 9 KJV)

Stop and think; what does "who art in Heaven" mean? What exactly does the word "heaven" mean? We tend to think of heaven as the dwelling place where our Lord God resides. Thus this statement means that our heavenly Father does indeed reside in that special placed called heaven.

As little children, we were told, "If you are not good, you will not go to heaven." This implies that heaven is a special place for only the good souls from here on earth. But God is the all-forgiving God, and his place in heaven is open to everyone who has reached the plane of perfection.

Jesus further said during his sermon, "Thy Kingdom come. thy will be done, in earth, as it is in heaven" (Matthew 6:10 KJV). Let the kingdom of God come more within the hearts of all men through the expression of love, joy, and understanding. We pray that the will of God may be done because we believe it to be perfectly loving and righteous. As it is in heaven, let each and every one of us express the goodness and mercy that the Lord God has instilled in us from conception, as we progress on this journey to heaven.

We each have our own conception of what we think heaven will be like. My grandmother Pendergast said that she would not meet up with her husband, as he had died so many years before her that he would have reached a different plane in his journey. When our mother was nearing death, I chuckled because when talking about death, she asked, "Do you think your dad will recognize me?" She knew her physical body would stay here on earth but her soul would enter heaven, and she hoped to be reunited with her husband. I read somewhere that all souls remain as a family unit regardless of how many times they return on this journey to perfection. This is such a warm and calming thought.

Look to the Heaven

What is the real purpose for our presence here on Earth? I tell you that we have a multifaceted purpose. We are to learn to give peace on Earth and goodwill to our brothers. Know that we are all in service to one another. Also learn to accept others' points of views and never bring harm to others.

We were given free will for a reason—to give us total control of self and prevent our being controlled by others. Many of us will not hold to this during this lifetime. Yet never forget there is always another tomorrow for us to make corrections. When we gain wisdom and love for all, our path to our true home will be opened by the light.

This was the writing for my poem "Look to the Heaven," first published in 2015 in *Spiritual Path to Wisdom*.

Look to the Heaven

Look to the heavens with overwhelming delight.
Then ponder when you may make this heavenly flight.
While this view from my window keeps me in awe,
Just think how it must be from a perch above it all.
The morning light is the beginning of time.
Without this brilliance, our sight would be blind.
Wait in patience for what's to come,
For it will work out and finally be done.

This appeared in our first book, *Spiritual Path to Wisdom*, in 2015.

Heavenly

We are this cup, now separate from the ocean,
Yet only for a brief interval of time, for time is always in motion.
No matter where this water is poured, it will always return to its source
Like a mighty river; all makes its way back to the sea, of course.
Never one drop of water either fresh or salty ever left this Earth.
Like this cup of water, we are looking for our true home in each rebirth.
When this dream is over in this world of illusion,
We will return the cup home for the final conclusion.
The oceans of this world are many, yet they are all joined together as one.
Whether fresh or salty, never has a drop been lost even by the sun.
Many times we may feel while on this Earth we are alone.
When the lessons of creation are learned, we will return to our true home.
My feelings are that the word "oneness" implies it could be two or even more.
All souls belong together in this heavenly ocean as their wings begin to soar.

Is a reflection of our oceans contiguous around this world we call Earth?
Do they exist not separately but in oneness? However, to me "oneness" means it could be two or many, so I choose the word "contiguous."

In heaven, all souls are blended together in a contiguous likeness. Take a cup of ocean water, for example. If someone was to ask you what it was, you would not say, "It is the ocean"; you would say, "It is from the ocean." Pour it back into the sea, and it is not separate any longer. Know this: everything you see on Earth is a reflection of the heavenly world. Therefore, I call seas the oceans of love and mercy.

Looking Aloft

Look up to the heavens, where the stars may block our view.
Yet look beyond them, and the stars will give way to blue.
Even farther we look, and behold, we are aware of twinkling of light.
The deeper we go in thought, the keener is our own insight.
It's so much brighter than the earth's own rising sun on the slope.
Off in the distance, this power of the light turns wishes to hope,
For at this moment, we know we have reached the heavenly heights,
Where self dwells as one with the heavenly Father, who is a great might.

Light

The unfolding of your words gives light; it
gives understanding to the simple.

—Psalm 119:130 (NIV)

The Attributes of Light

Light is a constant stream of energy of truth and knowledge. It never changes, for the truth of two thousand years ago is still the same today. This stream of knowledge is like a cable with a billion strands intertwined, each with a different purpose. When it comes in contact with one's universal mind of self, the one that is ready for this revelation, this light becomes your reality.

Much like radio waves or television, these waves come in contact and become sound and pictures. These waves are sent out only once, and if you miss them, they become lost, like a live program. Notice that these waves are straight lines that pass through matter: mud, steel, and even bricks. Light, however, is a steady stream forever. It never passes through matter but bends around objects and continues its bright path, creating a shadow. Because of the nature of light, it never enters the body. So this is proof that the universal mind is on the outside of the body. As such, the universal mind connects with light only when you are ready to receive the revelation. By choice of your free will, will you be able to accept this to your true self, which is within. This is proof that the true spirit of self is within our being and not in the cultural world. Know this: the universal mind is important, for without this connection to others with like minds, we could never react to each other or communicate. This togetherness is how we grow, learn, and love.

Brilliance of the Light of the Lord

There have been a large number of reports given by people who have had what is known as a near-death experience. Many of them report seeing a brilliant light in the distance that they are unable to seek or grasp. They find themselves returned to their physical bodies not at all certain of what just transpired. To be sure, such experiences have significant effects on these people, whether those effects be fear, wonder, or a desire to understand what just happened.

In Exodus 33:18–23 (NIV), we find this account of Moses interfacing with the Lord God on Mount Sinai:

> Then Moses said, "Now show me your glory." And the Lord said, "I will cause all my goodness to pass in front of you, and I will proclaim my name, the Lord, in your presence. I will have mercy on whom I will have mercy, and I will have compassion on whom I will have compassion. But," he said, "you cannot see my face, for no one may see me and live." Then the Lord said, "There is a place near me where you may stand on a rock. When my glory passes by, I will put you in a cleft in the rock and cover you with my hand (shield you) until I have passed by. Then I will remove my hand and you will see my back; but my face must not be seen."

Moses only saw the "Brilliant Light," which was the back of the Lord God. Is it possible that when someone has a near-death experience, he or she is also seeing only the back of God in all its brilliance? Could it be that it is not God's plan to have these people exit Earth at this time? God stated that anyone who sees his face will die. It makes sense that when we return to heaven at the end of this lifetime, we will then see the face of our Lord God. He is ready to welcome us home to the heavenly kingdom.

The light shows itself in many different ways; this is the effect it had on Moses: "When Moses came down from Mount Sinai with the two tablets of the covenant law in his hands, he was not aware that his face was radiant because he had spoken with the Lord" (Exodus 34:29 NIV).

Moses had seen the back of God, and he had personally spoken to our Lord. From that time forward, Moses had a brilliance about him that he often covered with a veil over his face.

There are many passages in the Bible about the Son of God, Jesus Christ, and the light that exuded from him. John 8:12 (NIV) states, "When Jesus spoke again to the people, he said, 'I am the light of the world. Whoever follows me will never walk in darkness, but will have the light of life.'" And Matthew 5:15 (KJV) states, "Neither do men light a candle, and put it under a bushel, but on a candlestick; and it given light unto all that are in the house."

Thus it is up to each and every one of us to let his or her light shine on those around us to make this a happier place. Remember: the light is a messenger sending us words of encouragement from our Lord God.

Let there be Light and there was Light

For the last six months, this phrase has kept popping into my mind at the oddest times, and I keep wondering why. This morning it came to me; perhaps I need to sit down and write about light!

When we think of light, we think the sun or turning on a switch to bring light into a room. But how about we dig a little deeper on this concept?

"Make my load light": We all carry around a lot of excess weight because of our own doing. Can we lighten the load to rid ourselves of guilt, an unforgiving heart, envy, or jealousy, to name just a few unpleasant traits? Just think how much happier we would be if just one or two of these traits were corrected. Life here on Earth will always be full of challenges, but that is when we must turn to our Creator and to our spirit guides to help us lighten the load.

"I feel light-headed": Do you feel this way perhaps because you stood up too quickly, or might there be a medical reason for this reaction? It might be because you are so full of happiness and joy that you are experiencing this sensation. If, for example, you won a lottery or a new car and you are simply beside yourself with excitement, that might cause you to feel light-headed and dizzy.

"Light up the room": Years ago, a candle might have illuminated your room. With today's technology, we only have to hit a button and the entire room is full of light. If you want to take a walk at night along a wooded path, you might bring along a flashlight to show you the way. Again, you need only push a button.

"Light the fire": Another meaning for "light" would be the act of using a match or piece of flint to start a fire—to light some wood. By lighting a fire, you would get not only warmth but also illumination, and thus light to be able to see.

"Light waves": These are a type of electromagnetic wave that are visible and can be seen as color by the naked eye. But light waves are a different type of wave, as they only go in a straight line and do not pass through solid mass, as radio waves do. Light rays can bend, thus causing us to see color, as in a rainbow. When a light wave is confronted by a person, building, or tree it cannot go through this mass but will bend and go around the object, thus causing a shadow to appear behind that object. Thus, we can say that light can also cause darkness, as in the case of a shadow.

"Enlightenment": Have you ever been sitting quietly and a voice in your head that told you something or made you aware? Did Moses not experience this on Mount Sinai when the Lord God spoke to him? I like to think such voices are your spirit guide giving you an opportunity to take action. When this revelation comes to you and you share this with others, you are giving others the opportunity to experience this and to be enlightened.

"Let there be light": "And God said, 'Let there be light'; and there was light. God saw the light, that is was good; God divided the light from the darkness" (Genesis 1:3–4 KJV). In the beginning, our world was in complete darkness. There was no button to push or candle to light, for all was darkness. Then our Lord God created the first day by dividing the light from the darkness, and he saw that it was good. If God had not created light, nothing on this planet would be able to grow, for plants and organisms need photosynthesis, which is the process of absorbing energy from sunlight to grow and mature. We have come to think of darkness as evil and light as goodness, but keep in mind that even at night the moon shines and gives us light. Darkness is necessary, as we need that time to rejuvenate our bodies and to rest. With the light comes a new day, and we are off and running to work, to school, or to church, or just to take part in the daily managing of our lives and the lives of our families. God gave us the gift of light, and so we must use it wisely.

"The light of life": "Jesus said 'I am the Light of the world: he that followeth me shall not walk in darkness, but shall have the light of life'" (John 8:12 KJV). Light represents the presence of the Lord God. Was it not the burning bush, which was light, that appeared to Moses? Everything is made up of light, and light is a powerful source of energy. Just as the sun gives energy to plants, the spiritual light gives energy to our souls.

Let There Be Light

And Lord God said, "Let there be light!"
What is this light that God created so bright?
This light began when he made all creation.
It started with nothing on that lonely station.
From plant, to water, to sky and so much more,
He knew what he had in mind for us—what was in store.
God's light seeks to bring us to a life of perfection.
He is talking about more than illumination.
What is this light God is talking about?
Has it a special meaning for those who are devout?
Light is a force sent from above.
God's light is this sign of his great love.

Light, Energy of Soul

This is very simple if you allow logic (the art of reasoning) to lead you to the truth. Out of nothing, where does light come from? I am not talking about the sun right now; I am talking about that light brighter than one thousand suns.

Everywhere you look here on planet Earth, there is light. Just think about this: our eyes see only light. I use the example of a tree to illustrate this. You stand at the shore of a large lake. Across the lake, a ranger is cutting down an oak tree in a campground. You see him swing his axe, and then a second later, you hear the impact. The reason you see the action first is that the speed of light is 186,000 miles per second, while sound travels at 740 miles per second. The conclusion, then, is that the tree and the ranger were in the light.

This force of light energy is nothing more than the soul. Not just one but millions and millions that make up everything you see. Of course, we are not now in the realm of simplicity. Let's go to the science of things. It has been proven that matter is nothing, yet no one is sure how it can become hard. This is where the spiritual side comes into play. The spiritual universal law is that thought creates an object and that the object is there forever—if, of course, it is maintained in accordance with the law of maintenance. In other words, you have to take care and maintain your possessions, whether these be your house, your car, or your garden.

Our eyes see only light, and therefore we see only soul, for everything is made up of soul. You may say, "Are you crazy?" But I ask you to look at how many millions of souls have passed over into the heavenly world; seen a powerful, soft, bright light; and never wanted to return back to Earth.

Now I ask you, where does this light come from? Where else but from the trillions of souls, and of course the heavenly Father and his master plan. Now, since the heavenly Father created all, and because Christ said, "I and the Father are One," so we as the sons of God have to be the light. If we are the light in the heavenly world, and we are, then why would we not be the light here on Earth, for Earth is but a reflection of heaven? Even the Lord's Prayer states this fact: "Thy Kingdom come, thy will be done in earth, as it is in Heaven" (Matthew 6:10 KJV).

Light—Spiritual

The following thoughts regarding light are spiritual—not based on what a person of science believes. When Jesus spoke to the people, he said, "I am the light of the world. Whoever follows me will never walk in darkness, but will have the light of life" (John 8:12 NIV). What is this light of life? Light represents the presence of the Lord God. Was it not the burning bush, which was light, that appeared to Moses? The Bible states, "God called the light 'day,' and the darkness he called 'night.' And there was evening, and there was morning--the first day" (Genesis 1:5 NIV).

I have said many times and shown via examples that everything is made up of light and light is a powerful source of energy. This is in the spiritual realm of creation, wisdom, and knowledge. I have said your eyes don't see; it is a universal mind that projects first, and then the eyes see.

I asked my Holy Spirit why this happens, and here is the answer I was given. Let's say there is a line of nine cars parked in a row. Each of the nine cars is different. Now, one hundred yards away, there are twelve people in a row, looking at the nine cars. So now the universal mind comes into play. The Mind sees and projects a thought to each person about each car in the line, so each person sees the same image a little differently. This is because the heavenly Father gave us each free thought to interpret what we see according to our background or our past history.

St. Bonaventure reminds us that when God declared that "light" is good, he was calling attention to the existence of yet another trilogy. As the cause of being, light is <u>powerful</u>; as the cause of understanding, light is <u>clear</u>; and as the cause of ordering life, light is <u>good</u>.

A personal note here: this is why I trust and love the spirit guides. When a revelation comes out of the blue, 100 percent on its own, and shows me knowledge to be shared, I praise the Lord for using me to enlighten this world. "Sometimes at that moment a wave of Light breaks into our darkness, and it is as though a voice were saying 'You are accepted. You are accepted, accepted by that which is greater than you, and the name of which you do not know'" (Paul Tillich, *The Shaking of the Foundation*).

Property of Light

Let's look at how the energy of light works. It passes through the air in silence, and not disturbing anything in its path. The important thing when it meets an object in its path is that it never enters the item but goes around it. For example, let's say that a beam of sunshine is aimed directly toward the front door of your house. If this light pierced this wooden front door and entered the house, it would light up the entire house. As long as the sun was shining, you would have light all day long. There would be no need for glass windows to let in the light, as you would already have light in the house. Now, if the day was cloudy or it was nighttime, there would be no light within this house.

Have you ever thought of where shadows come from? Let's say the light hits a dog walking in the park. It does not go through him but bends and goes around the side of the dog. But if you looked on the other side of the dog, you would see a shadow in the exact form of the dog. Shadows can be made only when there is light in front of the form. That is why on a sunny day there are lots of shadows but on a cloudy day there are none.

Our light comes directly from the sun, which is light years away. Now, this light has tremendous energy, as it can warm the planet, heat the oceans' water, melt the snow caps, and cause all vegetation to grow and mature. Without this light to make the plants grow so they can release oxygen so that you and I and the animal kingdom can breathe the breath of life, there would be no life. If our planet were in complete darkness with not a ray of light, this planet would become a ghost planet with no signs of life—plant, animal, or human.

After God created the earth and the heavens, what was the first element he needed to create so that this new planet could survive? "In the beginning God created the heavens and the earth. Now the earth was formless and empty, darkness was over the surface of the deep, and the Spirit of God was hovering over the waters. And God said let there be light ..." (Genesis 1:1–3 NIV).

Light Force

That light force of energy that puts the buzzing in your ear—
I have said before it keeps the body active year after year.
Our journey is complete for this cycle of residence.
This body is with us forever, as it is our eternal existence.
There are so many facets of life unseen in thought,
For that veil before us is so we are able to be taught.
If it were all laid out to see, it would just not be right.
We would be so overwhelmed, we could not gain insight.
We just need to have confidence that all will be well.
The plan is not for the present, but for generations to tell.
It is important to note that this plan is not only for self.
For within our reality, we want to include everyone else.

Shine Your Light

Do you shine your light straight ahead?
Do you then follow where you are led?
Or are you in control and determine where to go?
If this is the case, then your progress will be slow.
We are all God's children, and he knows our path.
He is our shepherd, so follow that awesome staff.
There is a plan set for each of us to follow, so let him lead.
We need to just trust in his guidance and do as he needs.
It is our heavenly Father who is the one in control.
Follow his direction, as his plan is to guide you and your soul.

Miscellaneous

We are not human being having a spiritual experience.
We are spiritual beings have a human experience.
Pierre Teilhard de Chardin

(1881 – 1955)

Free Will

This is a very complex issue, for to most it demonstrates that we believe we are self and that we stand alone with our own thoughts and mind.

The fact is that God the Creator, with the power to do anything, could have omitted free will and made us perfect from the start. Yet through his wisdom, God choose to give us free will—or, in another concept, free thought—to learn on our own, through various sets of laws of the universe. The cause and effect are that we earn perfection through good and bad choices. We experience these a thousand times in childhood. Our parents try to save us from mistakes, yet the real lessons come when we make mistakes and learn from them.

I have said many times that all events, causes, and effects on earth are reflections from above. "So God created man in his own image, in the image of God created he him" (Genesis 1:27 KJV). Believe me; the heavenly Father has no idea we experience pain, chaos, and sickness. God created Earth in concept only, start to finish, all perfect. It is through learning that humans create chaos, yet we see that when you follow the true path of universal laws in your life, the bad disappears and the effect is good! This statement alone tells you that pain and sickness and all other evil acts are just myths of wrong thinking of the mind.

"And God blessed them, and God said unto them, Be fruitful, and multiply, and replenish the earth, and subdue it: and have dominion over the fish of the sea, and over the fowl of the air, and over every living thing that moveth upon the earth" (Genesis 1:28 KJV). This tells us that our free will is the power here on Earth.

If God thought we could do this on our own, the Holy Trinity—Father, Son, and Holy Ghost—would not be with us 24-7. The only way to evolve into the perfect individuals we were created to be is through the guidance of our Holy Spirit, trusting the Lord and our own free will to make the correct choices.

Purging the Past

The past is gone and has no power at all in this present, for the cause and effect have been completed. You may retrieve the events through your brain memory, but they are over and done.

The human brain, not the universal mind, is the memory holder for the body. The brain has its illusion of power in the left side, which is the conscience, while the right is your spiritual unconscious mind. It stores nothing, for all that is truth and heavenly is there. In other words, it can never be fooled.

Let's say till age ten material negative thoughts or memories are near zero, so at age seventy-four, I have had sixty-four years of good and bad (evil). I now wish to purge from my brain all the negative thoughts and retain only the positive, spiritual types of perception.

Because your universal mind or spiritual self has power over the body, you can do this with ease. All you need to do is believe and ask for help. You already know how the body works: we eat food daily for energy, and our system processes the food, taking out the good and discharging the waste. You can do the same, if you believe, and start cleaning the brain of unwanted "dark matter." We have blood moving through the brain 24-7, and it then moves on through the body to be cleaned, so all you have to do is visualize all past negative memories and release them from the brain. As I said, this dark matter goes into the bloodstream and later is discharged from the body. Your brain is like a piano. With a piano, when you hit a key, it moves a wire that then vibrates and creates sounded. If I poke my finger with a needle, the same thing happens—a vibration moves via nerves to the brain to tell you your finger hurts. Now, because with Spirit you control the body 100 percent, you can control the brain to purge it. If I asked you to move your right arm over your head and you didn't want to, your arm would stay at your side. Please, please, please stop fooling yourself into thinking that the body has a mind of its own and you have no control over it.

This brain has great value if used correctly, but its only use is here in the present. Have you ever wondered why you can't remember your past lives? These memories are stored in your Holy Spirit—and with good reason. I once requested my Spirit to release these memories of past lives; in a flash I was overloaded with thousands of thoughts at once, and I honestly felt I was going crazy. In a moment, I asked it to stop. This was a lesson learned. Be careful what you wish for. Spirit let me know that everything will fall into place in time when I am ready.

When the brain is clear, your whole spiritual self will bloom, and your health and sight will change. How can you have pain if you are in control of the body and mind?

We, as spirit, have given our bodies the right to exist and to have all their attributes and human forms and functions. When we get sloppy and let down our guard, the ego (evil) can come into the body, resulting in poor health, pain, and sickness. To help fuel the fire, our televisions every day tell us we need drugs to stay healthy. It is time to take back the power and control. You, along with our spirit guide, your universal mind, your free will, and your free thought, are in complete control of this physical body. It is up to you to decide which path in life you want to take; will you follow your spiritual course or let your ego be in control?

Revelation

My goal for over thirty years has consisted of daily deep meditation and bringing forth my inner spirit guide. I want to allow others to find their own words and thoughts. It is important that our thoughts be our own from our inner self and not from chatter around us.

We live in a complex world both in thoughts and vision. Over time we have been programmed to see only material objects and not to appreciate the true nature of what is around us. I want you to quiet your mind so it is open to the reality of what is around you. This concept will enhance your everyday life and bring about happiness, joy, and great inner peace.

There are very few differences between the basic theories of the great religions of the world, for all are in evolution to bring joy and understanding to our lives. Unfortunately, many of these religions harbor small groups within particular sects that think killing and bombing are acts of their God. Christians in the fourteenth and fifteenth centuries were on this same path.

Many of my revelations are deep and thought-provoking; some are hard to get your mind around. I believe Earth is a reflection of what I call heaven in its own evolution. For this reason, I always ask Spirit for earthy examples. Spiritual understanding comes to us little by little.

I feel that I am a channel or conduit for the words from our heavenly Father to advance your thinking and lead you on the path to enlightenment.

Spiritual Enlightenment

I have read only one spiritual book other than the Bible. This one, *A Course in Miracles*, was over one thousand pages. I believe it was a slow read, which gave me the ability to understand the content. The first reading took over two years, starting in 1983. Then, in 1994, I read the entire book once again; I gained and absorbed additional insight. Then, in 2005, I again picked up this book and read it once again, and this time it took me a year and a half to complete it. With each reading, I gained further knowledge and understanding.

To my amazement, each time I read the book, it gave me a different perspective, for I was moving ahead on my Spiritual path. An example of this is what you learn as a young child of six years being so different from what you gain from that same lesson at the age of fifteen years.

Our minds absorb what we are ready for in our physical, mental, and spiritual growth. A further example of this is in Genesis chapter 1. Again, if you read this chapter at a young age and then ten or fifteen years later, the latter reading will leave you with a completely different understanding of the written word.

Reading, meditation and having a conversation with the Lord are so very important to our spiritual growth.

Spiritual Revelation

Whenever I speak to others about my spiritual revelations,
I always make clear that I am open to their interpretations.
There is always a thread of truth to all points of view.
Leave the door open for others' thoughts to review.
I pass the words and thoughts for everyone to gain,
Wisdom and knowledge are one and the same.
It's important, for all points of view are part of the game.
I have said before that thought forms travel through space.
They should be positive as they move from place to place.

The Art of Wisdom

What do I mean by the statement "We learn the art of wisdom?" We can read all we want to about lessons written or learned by others, and of course the study of the Bible as well. The art is that in the end you will allow your own opinions to surface and enter into your private space. You then find that the real truth lies within your own thoughts, not those of others.

Your revelations come in your own understanding and are stored in your mind in a picture form, for this is how your life exists—100 percent in the outer world. Remember: the outer self is the conscious or external self. We create forms every second, and this may have brought about the old saying "A picture is worth a thousand words." Remember: where we are in our spiritual development is the path our Spirit will take us. Down the road, we will change the pictures as we grow in understanding and wisdom.

Enlightenment never comes from others; someone else may spark the interest, but it is truly self that opens a new chapter in your life. Reading is a good thing if you are looking for a new thought to explore. Myself, I question everything, so I have a long list to work from. An example of this is Genesis chapter 1. Spirit has led me down a path to understand the total concept of creation. For others, they may see creation differently, and that is a good thing, for we are given only that which we will understand and that which will be helpful in our quest for perfection. This is what makes the Bible so powerful, for it shows us what we are reading in the now. Two thousand years from now, it will be even more powerful.

I have learned so much for a reason. Take the Holy Trinity, for example. We have the Father, the Son and the Holy Spirit. The Holy

Spirit is guiding this physical form of you and me. The Father and the Son are the higher belief in the heavenly world and the perfection of creation. Science and religion are slowly coming together to confirm that the creation of our planet earth had to be the work of a higher being. The reason the Lord Jesus Christ was given a physical form was so we as humans would believe in the higher power, for Jesus had a body just like mine and yours. Pray to any of these entities of the Holy Trinity, and your prayers will be answered in the time our Lord God wants them to be answered.

The Mind Signals the Brain

Look at the magic of your hands and the millions of nerves that run through them so you have control of them. It is the mind that controls how your hands function. A signal is sent from your mind to your brain to perform a certain task.

Allow me to use the example of a primitive man who has an idea to construct a shelter. Using his hands, he takes mud, grass, tree limbs, and his imagination, and behold, a hut is constructed. During his time on Earth, he may build many of these huts for survival as he forages from place to place. He then passes this knowledge on to his children so they can take over this task in the future. A few generations later, one expands on the concept of a hut and, via evolution, constructs a more solid hut of stones, mud, a palm-frond roof, windows, and a door using this same principle of the mind telling the brain of an idea and the hands performing the task.

In today's modern world, this exact method of creation and expansion of various things still holds true. Yet because we live in a time of heightened consciousness, we know that from day one everything will become obsolete and the next generation, with more imagination and knowledge, will enhance things. So, we are in an ever-changing world.

The extremities of the human body—the hands, legs, and feet—are useless without our minds telling our brains what functions we want to do. Whether we want to walk, speak, or develop a new invention, the mind and brain must work together for the end result. The Lord God created Adam; he created man as a physical being, and he imparted to him a free will to discover and expand our thinking.

Wait and Sea

You can walk on water, and you called me to follow you into the sea. I swam out and I followed you. I swam out too far, and I was scared, always asking for reassurance and guidance. You continued to tell me to believe. You stepped farther, and I swam farther. I found myself in the unknown depths of the sea.

The storm came in like a hurricane. The waves threw me over, and the currents held me down. I fought against the storm, as I thought this was the only way of survival. I fought until the storm took it all from me. It took my pride. It took my anger. It took my envy. It took my doubt. The storm fed off my sins; I was only fighting myself. I surrendered. I let go, and I let God.

As I let go, the storm rolled out, and I found myself surrounded by a calm sea. I was somewhere new. Peace, light, and faith kept me afloat as I surrendered to the Son. "Just wait," he whispered into the depths of my heart. "Just wait right here, be still." I treaded water. I slowly moved my arms and gracefully kicked my legs as I felt the embrace of the calm around me. Not looking for land, not following the stars for direction, I did not know what was to come, but I believed I was saved.

I continued to tread. Growing tired, I felt the claws of control attempting to place their prideful reins around my heart. He whispered, "Just wait. It's coming." This was my test. Was I going to selfishly take control or faithfully surrender? I continued to tread. The depths of the sea became my endurance, my fuel, my strength, and my energy. Just then, I felt it! On the most beautiful day, I felt the message of the breeze. "Get ready."

I know! I feel it! I know it in the core of my soul! It's coming! It's more than I ever imagined and bigger than my hopes and dreams. It's my destiny, my passion, and my purpose. I can't see it yet, but I felt the breeze that begins to stir the sea. The wave is just beyond the horizon. I can feel it. I will continue to tread water and listen as it begins to form. I am meant to catch this wave. I swam through the storm to shed the weight of myself. I released them like anchors that sank to the bottom of the ocean floor. I am going to catch this wave and ride it in to where God intends me to be.

Angeline A. Piskorski
October 23, 2013

Oneness

I am one with my father and the universe.
I am one with mother earth.
I am one with everyone within the reach of my voice.
And, in this togetherness, we ask the divine intelligence
to eradicate all negatives from our hearts, from our minds,
from our words, and from our actions.
And, so be it.

—Babatunde Olatunji
(1927–2003)

I Am One with Many

This is a subject that is hard to get your mind around, for we are all self, or one person. I am speaking for myself. I have a name to separate this person from others. I have a mind of my own and free will of my own. So how is it that I am considered one?

People often say to me, "Do I have to give up my beliefs and turn it over to a universal mind, or what some people call God? Is it like follow the leader, and will I lose my sense of self? The answer is emphatically no!

The universal law says we are all connected. Everything we do affects others. When we have good thoughts of love, joy, and happiness, this affects those around us. But if our thoughts and expressions are of hate, sadness, or anger, that too affects us all. Thus, we are one body affected by many.

When we have earned the right to return to a heavenly place and our thoughts are pure, we will have this same feeling of oneness multiplied thousands of times.

$\mathcal{I}$ and the Father Are One

Christ said many times, "I and the Father Are one" (John 10:30 NIV). I know that some people have a hard time with the thought that when they rise to heaven, they are giving up self. The ego wants to remain as self so it can be different and unique. But that is not the way in the heavenly world; there all are one.

The easiest way to understand this is through the example of a cup of water taken from the ocean, put in a vase, and placed on the mantel. You do not tell your friends and family that this is "the ocean." You also know that you have not reduced the power of the vast ocean by removing this one cup of water. But keep in mind that the little cup of water on your mantel has no power at all. Now, if you take that little cup back to the ocean and release it to allow it to once again become part of the vast ocean, it again gains power and strength.

Now suppose a man who has been homeless and lost here on earth should die. His soul will find its way to heaven. By himself this person had no power, but when his soul arrives in heaven, he is united with all the other Souls and he now has great power.

When one dies, the soul from within ascends to the heavenly world. It knows the route and needs no direction. Similarly, the ocean and river waters know the route and where to flow. Take a heavy rainstorm with all its drops of water falling to the earth. The water may flow into a ditch, then to a river, and finally back to the ocean.

When the soul arrives in heaven, it becomes part of the whole or it becomes one with all the other souls in heaven. Just like the water in the rivers, lakes, and oceans, it all returns to the one source to become one.

Importance of Oneness

Regarding the water on this planet, there is not one drop more or one drop less now than when the earth was formed billions of years ago. Earth is enclosed; nothing can be added to it, and nothing can be taken from it.

Soul is exactly the same. When we say, "We are all one," that refers to soul's past, present, and future, for we don't realize it, but the earth is living in the now. "Thy kingdom come. Thy will be done in earth, as it is in heaven" (Matthew 6:10 KJV).

Like the water, every soul that will ever be on Earth for over thirteen billion years is already here in one form or another, working its evolution. Knowing this, we are all perfect, yet we have not reached that point. But as one we will. The giver is God, and we will grow into perfection.

Genesis Chapter 1 tells it the way it is; Earth was completed in six days, changeless in every way. It is only our perception that makes it seem different. Resting occurred on the seventh day not because God was tired but because the seventh day is the now, when perfection exists.

What we need to do as humans is look beyond what we see with our eyes. Knowing that the eyes don't see all, it is the mind that creates the image first, and then the eyes see. The big step for everyone is to stop and go to your inner world and ask for a revelation via your guide to show you a simple truth. You will find that daily, while you sit and are quiet, new answers will come and things will make better sense, to your own amazement. It takes a little practice to guide the mind. You can never shut it down, for the law is that it works 24-7, but you can get it on your side.

Discovery is in our nature; we just have to know how to tap

this source. These intelligent laws are meant to be used. Just ask for knowledge and guidance. That is why we have these spirit guides within. They are just waiting for you to wake them up. During your whole life, they have been helping you, so bring them to the front now. Get in touch with your inner self and use your spirit guide to help you. Become one with our heavenly Father.

Law of Divine Oneness—Universal Law

We are all one. We are connected and part of the whole. What this means is that all of mankind, all of nature, and all of God is one.

We are like Adam and Eve, created by God, so we are all one. God created us in his image and likeness; therefore, we are one.

Because this is true, then every thought, feeling, speech, or action relates to and affects others. We need to recognize the good we see in others, as this is a direct reflection of our self. These positive vibes are sent out as energy, bringing us nearer to God and to our ultimate self.

As we put this universal law of divine oneness into practice, we experience a closer bond and connection with our heavenly Father. Remember: good thoughts and actions result in good things coming your way.

Miracle of Oneness

The true miracle of creation is the Creator's Spirit, which made the laws we must all follow—not the man-made laws, but the spiritual laws. If not for these laws, how could we be one? It would be impossible. Here is the reason we would be in trouble without a single, or universal, mind.

If we each created our own earth, one person may want oxygen and desire it to be 10,000 feet above sea level. Another person may desire oxygen 250 feet below sea level. One would live, and the other would die. It is the same scenario with water. If one preferred fresh water the other preferred salt water, how confusing it would it be for the soil. If you planted a seed and watered it with salt water, that would surely cause it to die.

I feel it best not to question or ask how the millions of laws work. We can, however, see and respect how the laws do work, and use them to our benefit. Respect fire, for it has great value yet it can hurt you. In its evolution, mankind discovers new laws, though really it is like I have said before—that God created the concepts of the future (e.g., electricity and steel). We only need to discover it, not understand how it was created.

One, Never Two

A few days ago, I wrote my daughter Tracy a note stating that seeds have knowledge, for they know exactly what they are. A tomato is never a cucumber or a beet. She was overwhelmed by this revelation of mine. So let's go deeper.

We have to look at the whole picture. As humans, we all have a common mind, for if we were not connected in one mind, then we could not communicate with one another. But let's not forget we were given the great gift of free thought so that we could control our own lives; nothing happens unless we allow it. This connection of mind is because we and they are one.

I will again use the example of the ocean. You can never separate it throughout the world. Sure, you can take a cup of water out of it and years later return it. It will blend right back in to be part of the whole one. When you removed it, did the ocean lose power or change at all? The answer is no.

Let me bring you back to the seed. Every seed in the world knows what it is, and therefore a seed may become an oak tree. Once it starts the germination process, it will never be the same and will change as it grows. Perhaps someday it will be made into lumber, fuel for a home, wood chips for a garden, or compost for mother earth. Everything follows the same path as we mature, age, and die.

Another example is coal and oil deposits; these are a perfect example of how things change over billions of years. They have evolved into something very different from what their original matter was. Without evolution, this planet and humans would not grow in maturity. The discovery of coal and oil alone required many men of one mind working to come up with a use for these two products.

If one wants to think that all forms of plant life, mineral deposits, or animal life have no knowledge of what they are, fine. Would it then make sense that during the start of creation, only humans would evolve and not all things? An oak tree three billion years ago was only four inches tall, so thus it grew and evolved into the tree we have today. So, if the plant world evolves, it makes sense that we humans also evolve and work together as one being, because my Father in heaven created all things on this planet. "I and the Father are One" (John 10:30 NIV).

Oneness

The reason the subject of oneness is hard is that we on earth are all about self. What is self? Self is a person's essential being that distinguishes him or her from others.

Every religion in the world has its own god, and of course all of them have different names and writings to go along with their beliefs. Christians have the Bible, Christian Scientists have Mary Baker Eddy, the Jews have the Torah, and the book for Islam is the Koran. All of these have the same thread of truth but at the same time are different. All these books are open to different interpretations, so I find it best to get my information from within or from the Holy Spirit.

I believe that everything we see with these human eyes has absolute intelligence and gives off light via the energy of the soul. I make this statement because I see light in everything I view, so I know it to be true. Our Creator has given each of us the gifts of life, soul, love, heart, light, and eyes so that we may live our lives as one with him. Remember: you do not have a soul; you *have* a body, but you *are* a soul.

The sage Rabindranath Tagore said, "I see light in everything, Bright when perfect, Dull when in progress."

That said, all objects you see then are also just one, for they are all the same and fool us because they have different shapes, and of course we give them various names, such as "table," "chair," "car," etc. Objects in different forms have reasons here on earth, but you all know that when you pass on, not one thing you see with your human sight goes with you.

Another example of absolute intelligence is the story I tell of the tomato seed that you plant in the garden. You water it, and the bacteria in the soil eat away the seed's outer husk, and when it gets to the inside, the live part, it stops and the inner seed breaks through the ground surface. This is the beginning of the growth of the tomato plant.

The universal mind is in play regarding oneness of the outer self, for it is the center of intelligence to all souls. Every time you think or dream on the inner self, you set in motion the act of creation. Remember: free will is within, and for our dreams to become reality, they have to move to the outer self; then we can recruit other souls to help construct our creation via their universal mind.

Because of the oneness of all minds, which the Creator designed, one cannot contradict another. Jesus Christ said it best: "Go! It will be done just as you believe it would" (Matthew 8:13 NIV). This is proof that if one word has power, then the law is that all words have the same power, so speak with care. Universal law does not ever choose; it sets the rules only and knows not the outcome. As an example, electricity can heat your house while at the same time burning your dinner; it knows not.

Think of it this way: God is our creator. He is the Father and created us in his image and likeness. He is not many but only one—not two or more Gods. And God said to Moses, "Thou shalt have no other Gods before me" (Exodus 20:3 KJV). All this really means is that there is to be only one God. That said, how could we not be one with one another, for we are all from the same cloth.

If we, as soul, are not one with one another, how can we be the perfect image of the one God. Free will was not given to us to make us separate but to allow us to be in control of our own thoughts so we could think, learn, and gain wisdom not as a puppet but as a thinker finding his or her way home.

People think that in giving up self they are losing something and will lose the power of thought. This is wrong, for when you join all others as one, as did the Lord Jesus Christ, you become one with God. How could that be a bad thing? Is God not creating every day? God sees us every day in secret; you don't see God, but you know he is there.

The sage Rabindranath Tagore said, "You cannot possess God. The mystery remains endless all the days of your life. But you can feel it inside and cherish that feeling like a precious pearl. We are all mysteries to ourselves, and when we start to think, we are eavesdropping on messages sent from above."

The riddle of the apparent separation between God and man is the mystery of what makes self think it is not one. You must know that we are eternal beings and have been given free will, so we have the power of thought to dream of the unknown, working daily to move ahead toward a divine center, knowing deep down that upon acceptance of oneness we will return to the source of creation and love will overwhelm us as we enter the gates of eternity.

The sage Rabindranath Tagore also said, "God has to be a mystery because the only one who could explain him is himself, and no one bothers to ask him anymore."

Everything about human existence, including love, death, truth, and beauty, needs the foundation provided by God. God justified the mystery of life. He gave human beings a soul and a lord to surrender to.

Oneness

Tell me, how can we all be one when we seem blind and sightless?
If you get to know your neighbors better, you will see a likeness.
Only when we keep our self separate do we feel alone.
Through the universal mind, we feel connected and really belong.
We are all busy in this world trying to get things done.
We forget that together the path is easier and can be fun.
This world we perceive seems so real, with friends to console,
Yet it is just made up for our ego to try to control.
The reality is, we have to change our thinking and change sides.
By turning within and seeking, we find our spirit guides.
Either your ego controls or it finds the pathway to peace.
The course is hard, but with truth and love, you will find release.
Ego's plan is to keep you on the dark path to deception.
The heavenly world looks for happiness and love with no exception.

We Are One

Without question, the concept that we are one is nearly impossible to comprehend here on this planet Earth. The reason is that from the moment we are born, we are thinking of the self. You come into this world kicking and crying, for you are scared that the self will be harmed. You leave that nice, cozy, warm place in your mother's body to be thrust into the cold.

As we grow and mature, there are many lessons we must learn. Life is not all about self, as there are others in this world and we must learn to share and become a part of the group, family, or community.

With age, most of us learn to depend on self for all the material things around us. Self must get a good job, a new car, a house, and lots of other material possessions. With this background, it's hard to believe that we are one with each other. This concept is so ingrained in our thinking; why should we give up all that we have worked hard for? How, then, do we take this giant step to move forward and think of ourselves as one? The Bible states, "I have given them the glory that you gave me, that they may be one as we are one" (John 17:22 NIV).

Let's start with the Bible: "For God so loved the world that he gave his one and only Son ..." (John 3:16 NIV). With that truth in mind, I, being God's child, am also his son, and this makes us one. It's not really a bad thing, for in the heavenly world, everything is perfect; therefore, all thoughts have to be one thought that is also perfect.

In the past, I have stated that we need examples to explain this theory. Let me use the example of the sports event where fifty thousand fans are all sitting in the bleachers, wishing and praying for the home team to win. This is known as home-field advantage. It is true that a team plays better because of the energy from their fans. If you are there and cheering, you are one with all those people rooting for the home team. When the game is over, you go home and the old feeling of self returns; so instead of one, you are now self.

Remember how after 9/11, all the people across the country came together to stand up and support the United States of America. There was strength and conviction that we as a country were one. It is so important that we all continue to keep those positive thoughts at the forefront of our minds.

This is another example I have used before, but it works: Ocean water is vast and covers two-thirds of the earth and has great power. This water is melded together with no voids of its own; it is just one big mass of liquid. Take a bucket of water out, and the ocean is still the ocean; take this pail of water home and keep it covered, and the next year you can take it back to the ocean and pour it back in. The result is that it blends back in as if it never left. We are that bucket, and in time we will be carried back to our true home of perfection as if we never left.

Maybe, just maybe, we are not yet ready to embrace this concept in this lifetime. Maybe this tool of evolution is preparing us for oneness in little, tiny baby steps. I, for one, respect all forms of living things and will catch a spider in my house and return it to the outdoors. Many say I am crazy, but I respect life because we are all one.

There is a reason for Earth having undergone thirteen billion years of evolution, with another five billion to go to gain knowledge and wisdom on the road to perfection. Just think how far we have come in the last few hundred years just with all the new technology at our fingertips.

I believe that the attitudes of marriage and love for your offspring are the path set by evolution for us to acknowledge that we are all one. It is our job as parents to lead by example for our children to respect everyone and all things. It is important to respect that dog walking down the street or the pretty little girl sitting alone in the candy store. We are all one and thus must treat everyone as God would want us to.

We do see oneness every day in our daily lives. While driving your car, you allow someone else to go first, you hold the door open for the someone behind you, or you just simply smile as you pass someone on the street.

The reason this subject is so hard is that we here on earth are all about self. What is self? The internet definition says it is "a person's essential being that distinguishes them from others." What is oneness? It is a state or condition of perfect harmony or accord.

I believe that in time we will all understand that oneness is not the giving up of self but rather a method whereby we all think in perfection and love with no boundaries. This means correcting our thought process to reflect God's wishes that we were all created in his image and likeness.

We have heard many times of people who have crossed over the River Jordan and come back; they always exclaim on the power of the heavenly light and the feeling of bliss. The reason for this is the reality that there is one thought and one mind, and this power of light is the energy of souls as one. We give up nothing to gain everything. Our day will come; it's been promised.

There is only one God, the Creator of the heavens and the earth and of all mankind, manifested to mankind as Father (creator), Son (savior), and Holy Ghost (dwelling within). Like Jesus, we are God's children, and as such, we are all one.

We Are One

We are all one—you and I and all the people around.
We are all created as one, as our sameness will abound.
The sense of self is developed from the time of conception.
Everything about us is me—me, mine—mine without exception.
Our job in maturity is to learn that we are all one.
"I and the Father are One"—as stated by the Father's Son.
In major catastrophic events, we all pray and work together.
It may be during a storm, or at church or other places we gather.
There are also examples of oneness through our daily lives.
Think of others to help, to assist however you can derive.
Thinking of others before self is a prime example
Kindness and love, expressed to everyone, are so simple.
Our heavenly Spirit will be sure we do not lose one sole.
We are one: one mind, one body, one soul.

John 10:30 (NIV): "I and the father are One."

Planet

Earth is the holiest place in the Universe,
loving the earth, and loving life is the
way to generate positive vibrations

—Amit Ray, philosopher and spiritual master
(1960 -)

Complexity Made Simple

As a horticulture buff, I always use the example of a tree when I try to make a point. It is a creation of billions of years ago that changed from a four-inch-tall tree to the stately one-hundred-foot tree we see today.

Science to this day has no idea how water, via osmosis is taken in from the roots and then, against gravity, via a paper-thin layer just under the bark to the top of the tree. This is what scientists call capillary action. Yet in their laboratories they only get the water to move upward a foot at best. It is interesting to note that the first recorded observation of capillary action was by Leonardo da Vinci during his lifetime (1452–1519).

When God created the tree and all other objects on this planet earth, never did he create other laws, such as the law of gravity. In other words, the tree was surrounded by a vacuum to allow water to travel to the top leaves of this hundred-foot tree.

Like Earth, which travels through space at six thousand miles per hour, never a strong wind do we feel on our face. Nor does the spinning cause us to fall off the planet and into the atmosphere.

Yes, the creation of this planet earth was a very complex event. But as with the laws of nature and the universal laws, everything has a cause and an effect.

Complexity

While we think and talk out loud, plants and animals do communicate not only to each other but also to us. Let's take the young sapling in the yard as an example. If you fail to water this sapling, then what will you see? Nonverbally, the plant is telling you its leaves are wilting and it needs water.

You can train your pet to learn certain commands, such as "sit," "stay," and "down." Either by verbal expression or a hand command, the animal will obey.

Our world is complex, but there is a form of communication between all living things.

This writing and the poem "Complexity" first appeared in my book *Spiritual Path to Wisdom*, published in 2015.

Complexity

I wonder at the complexity of what I see.
I will use the example of a tree.
In the forest it grows stately and tall.
It may not have a voice for us to hear at all.
Yet in reality it gets its great power through nature,
For within this tree it has strength from its maker.
The secret of nature for its voice is not sound.
It knows without water its leaves will turn brown.
So just sit back and enjoy what you see,
For in truth this tree is much like me!

Creative Law of Discipline

Your mother and father taught you discipline as you grew up. This in turn made you a better person. This planet, via the Creator, has set universal laws to be followed. So, when you break these laws, the law we all know as cause and effect is in play. We don't know many of these laws on the conscious level, but they are still there. This is why sometimes events happen over and over again in different ways to show us how to get something right.

Some disciplines are not easy and can be downright painful, yet we learn, and many times we look back and say, "That was a good thing." Remember: with your freedom of thought, on the unconscious level you okayed this discipline to happen. Many a time when bad things come your way, you might say it is bad Karma from another lifetime. Is it really Karma, or did you act in a way that is in opposition to the universal laws of our planet? Remember that cause and effect always come into play. You make a decision, and that is the cause, and you must be prepared for the effect.

Spirit has all the wisdom, so place your trust in the Holy Spirit.

$\mathscr{E}$arth

First off, it must be understood that this is my belief. I look at God much in the same way I looked at my own father. He loved me as well as the whole family. In fact, he had the same respect for all souls that he met.

With this said, I believe that the heavenly Father would never hurt his creations, and I doubt honestly that God is aware of the chaos here on Earth. Secondly, I don't believe that we, as humans, ever left the heavenly world. We are here only in thought, given a body with the purpose only of getting us around. For without direction from our Spirit via thought, this body is powerless.

Answer this question: Would you as a parent take your children and throw them under a bus, or drown them and put them in harm's way? Of course not, so why would you think a loving God would cause all this chaos on Earth?

In brief, let's look at Genesis after he rested on the seventh day. "And God saw everything that he had made, and, behold, it was very good" (Genesis 1:31 KJV). And then let us look further: "Thus the heavens and the earth were finished and all the host of them" (Genesis 2:1 KJV).

With the above done in totality, now we move on to Genesis 1:26 (KJV). "And God said, Let us make man in our image, after our likeness: and let them have dominion over the fish of the sea, over the fowl in the air, and over the cattle, and over all the earth, and over every creeping thing that creepeth upon the earth." Now, I have written this before many times. Humans have the power to create, for God gave us this tool, as we were formed in his image and likeness. One soul has the power, but think of thousands or millions of souls all with the same thoughts. Take a baseball game with all the fans cheering for the home team. The players feed off this power of thought to go on to win on their home field. People living in the Midwest are afraid of winds and tornadoes, and the millions focus on and behold the storms. This, of course, is not a pleasant thought—that the power of thought can kill and destroy life. Remember: millions of good things happen with this same power of thought. Miracles happen every day when people pray for individuals or events. The sun rises and sets, and trees take in carbon dioxide and discharge oxygen for all living creatures. If they didn't discharge oxygen, there would be no plant life. This is the evolution of everything here on planet earth.

This brings us to where we are today, so let's regress, say, 125 years, which is not that far when you recall that the earth is thirteen billion years old to date. In the year 1890, we were riding in horse-drawn carriages, there were no phones as of yet, and candles provided light for our rooms. Look where we are today, with the lightning speed of radio waves. We have global networks, and old age has gone from fifty to seventy-five-plus years. This world is on the fast track of development.

Now, see how this reality is working. Our complex body is the engine for all this growth. Doctors, via science, are copying the body's organs and of course trying to figure out the brain. Keep in mind that the brain is a physical organ but the mind is a spiritual entity. Man is trying to make computers work like the brain. The body with all its complexity is like the mirror that the research-and-development departments in large corporations are working on for new discoveries.

The complexity in this world was God's plan to move us along in evolution. If there was not a blueprint in front of us, it would not be present today. I have said for years that God's plan was in concept only, for he wants man to expand via his mind. Science states that our body's brain is used at perhaps only 15 percent of its capability. Just think how things might change as our brain reaches even greater capacity.

The most important point in this writing is this: There is nothing in God's creation that was not designed for expansion via the thought process. Also, nothing was created that was not for the purpose of serving man. Think about this: we are in service 100 percent for one another; there is not a profession out there that is not in service to our brothers. Via the complexity of everything, this forces us to move ahead, for that was why we were given free will.

When you really think about it, the body is our own universe and it is our lesson to learn to control via our mind. It really is our slave and has no power unless we direct it. Complexity creates the concept to solve and move on to evolution, which is ahead for all things.

Earth Journey

We all question what our role is during this earthly stay.
It's to grow in consciousness, and that's the only thing in play.
When we grow in consciousness, we are fully aware of our actions.
Whereas in the past, we were unaware of all negative reactions.
Those who create chaos and pain—are they aware what they created?
To them greed, chaos, and pain are simply a way of life and never debated.
Lifetime after lifetime, we all grow and mature,
For then the ego's footprint becomes less and less for sure.
Wisdom is the method of learning whereby we respect all living things.
We become aware that all life has feelings, and we see the love they bring.
The power of heaven is oneness, but not with individual thought,
For the creator allows creation by advancement and freedom taught.
Look to your brothers who have different views and perceptions.
Yet we are one with respect to their thoughts, but not deception.
One can think differently, yet one's thoughts are dear,
For in the end, our goals are the same and very clear.
When we grow and learn via our own positive actions,
We are teaching our brothers to have similar reactions.
We travel this path, passing each and every planned station.
This journey is good, as it exceeds all our expectations.

Earth's Upheaval

In the beginning, the earth was in a major upheaval.
This was the start of a cause and effect of good and evil.
While the mountains grew and the oceans warmed,
It was time for life, and the amoeba was born.
The amoeba's coming was to produce oxygen in the sea.
This opened the door for aquatic life, you see.
As wild life grew in abundance on the ground,
The cycle of evolution now began to be found.
Now this intelligent design was ready for man.
The totality of creation had started to expand.
Some say coincidence of perfection at its best;
I say it's a miracle—the master plan laid to rest.

Far Country Reality

Today's lesson here on earth is that reality comes via what we see with our eyes, yet it is thought that creates what the eyes see.

We all want to experience the far country, and because our earth-plane experiences occur via the eyes, we expect the same result in our visits to these higher planes. This is wrong for the newcomers; this is why we don't remember our journey to the heavenly worlds, for we don't see there. We experience it only through the method of thought.

Today's revelation this morning came to show me this fact. It's believed by the newcomer that he or she will see via his or her earthly eyes the wonders of heaven and will remember when he or she returns. This is wrong. In time, when you are deemed ready, you will see with your spiritual eye and remember in detail. But before I share the far country, know that this is how sight works on the earth plane:

1. Thought, via mind, creates what you see and observe.
2. Seeing sends back to mind what it sees—of course with a judgment.

Via your freedom of thought, you send back to the eyes exactly what you, as Spirit, believe. If your judgment was negative, that is what you will create and see. If it is positive, that will be the result. It is all in your control. In other words, you make up your reality as you go along. Don't forget that there is another factor here, and it is called universal mind. This I have to dig deep to explain, for you have to remember that with free will, we can accept or reject all that is in front of us. As I have written many times, space is covered with thought forms and we can take out of space the ones we want. As an example, New York City exists via these thought forms via the universal mind. Here on the West Coast, we don't see these forms, but if you travel to the East Coast, you tap into these and New York City is seen via your mind and eyes.

These statements above are why 95 percent of the people say, "I will just live my life via what I see and leave the method of how it happens to others."

True vision comes not from your two eyes but from your spiritual third eye, called the *Tisra Til*. This is the seat of the soul and the place where we gently and calmly focus our attention in meditation. It is located just above the nose and between the two eyes. This true vision is an experience that can never be described. Because it is true reality, one would never dream of judgment there. How do you get to this point of stillness, silence, and focus of the immortal self within? Don't expect vision, but think only of thought. At first you will think you are making it up on your own. This is not true, for your thoughts will take you on a journey you could not have made up. It is human nature to doubt yourself, for when we try to reach these heavenly worlds and don't, we feel that maybe we are not worthy, and this is wrong. Never let your mortal mind (evil) try to convince you of this.

Once when I was in the far country, I was in a large room with thousands of souls. The teacher was up front in street clothes, clean shaven. While we all had respect for this person, we listened. In the next moment, this being, changed on stage to a person with a beard, no shoes, and a white robe. At that moment, the whole crowd changed, for we knew we were in the presence of the Master, Jesus Christ. The lesson here is that looks can fool you but reality never can.

In the Beginning

Why is Creation important? The reason is that once you understand a small part of Creation, you will then find an avenue of wisdom and understanding of the following:

1. Spirit—the heavenly Father that encompasses every facet of you and me.
2. Soul—our higher self with the goal of evolution through perfection with the help of our spirit guide.
3. Body—the vessel that exists just to get us around this planet earth, powered by thoughts of soul and of spirit.

Over the years, science and religion have moved closer together, whereas in the beginning they disagreed on everything.

Let us look at how the higher power we call by different names created the complexity of Earth and the universe in only six days.

Step 1: Billions of years ago, God created the building blocks for life—things man would need to survive. First things first, the planet needed water, air, soil, and sunshine to survive by itself alone. Man would need all this plus a body and all its complexity to operate.

Step 2: This then became the starting point for evolution. Plant life started slowly, for rich soil had to evolve. The same is true of the oceans and the seas. From simple amoebas to insect life to creatures in the sea, life began to form on this planet earth.

Step 3: Animal life matured from single-celled organisms to organisms with trillions of cells via evolution. Planet earth now had saber-toothed tigers, dinosaurs, birds of prey, and various creatures in the sea.

Step 4: With billions of years under its belt, this planet called Earth was now ready for the introduction of man.

Step 5: God gave man the edge over all, because he was gifted with free will and dominion over all. Man was given the ability not only to know but also to know that he knows. Man was then born to be a cocreator with the Holy Spirt.

Step 6: This was just the beginning of the steps that mankind would take. Man, quickly learned to provide a hut for shelter from the weather and from the wild animals that roamed the earth. He later discovered that tools needed to be made to forage for food, clothes needed to be constructed to protect the body's heat, and on and on. The primitive man evolved. Hundreds of years later, this man evolved in his thinking to develop the auto, the wheel, and the airplane, as well as to travel into space.

Now, it would truly be foolish to compare the complexity of today's world to that of the caveman, or simply to think that in the thousands of years ahead, we would look and act like our forefathers and live as they did.

Even more of a waste of this planet earth's evolution is the belief that, on the road to enlightenment, there is a being behind us that we call the past. That said, the same holds true for what many call the future. Souls are thus behind us and in front of us.

If this were not true and all humans live only once, why is ours a universe of billions of years of past and more billions of years of future?

Food for thought: The simple creation of the wheel has, via thought, moved to air travel. God needed to create only one variety of tree with the complexity of its structure, and billions have evolved from that. The cave evolved to the homes of today, all via the thoughts of man.

God creates new souls every day in this classroom called Earth.

Miracle of Air

Air, like everything else here on earth has rules to follow per universal laws. As an example, you will notice air is never heated by the sun; rather, it is heated by material objects that absorb the sun's rays and give off warmth into the air. These objects are roadways, bridges, buildings, and even rocks. If you go to a mountaintop, the air is cooler, and the air in outer space is quite fridge. Even if you sit under a shade tree, the air is cooler as well.

The air around us is subject to the pull of gravity as well. Let's take a tornado whirling through the sky as an example. The gravitational pull of this majestic force wants to pull it to the ground. Another example would be smoke from a fire, for though it rises into the atmosphere, in reality it rises as the result of the heat of the fire. Heat is lighter than air. Have you ever noticed that the air at your ceiling is much warmer than the air in the rest of the room?

At times, air can almost be considered a solid. Try putting your arm out of the window of the car when you are driving down the road at sixty miles per hour. Doesn't it feel like something solid has hit smack against your arm? How about trying to open a door during a hurricane and feeling that forceful rush of solid air pushing your body backward.

Another of the wondrous qualities of air is that it carries oxygen so we humans can breathe. The carbon dioxide in air sustains the plant life on this planet, which in turn emits oxygen into the atmosphere. Where does this carbon dioxide come from but from the animals and humans that exhale this precious commodity with every breath?

The miracle of air is that it has the ability to mix with water so that billions of life forms can live. Even the waters of the oceans and lakes contain air. The same miracle occurs where air and water mixes in the soil to support life. "The wind blows wherever it pleases. You hear its sound, but you cannot tell where it comes from or where it is going. So it is with everyone born of the Spirit" (John 3:8 NIV).

Miracle of Birth

When one thinks of birth, one immediately thinks of a baby being born. Yet in this universe there are many different forms of birth.

Let's take a vegetable seed as an example. It will germinate when you add water and put the seed into the moist, rich soil. But then the bacteria begin to eat the dead, hard shell, which is the covering around the live seed. You will note the bacteria stops at the live part of the seed. The law of nature knows that the bacteria are not to eat the soft green center, which will grow and become the plant.

Now think about the birth of oxygen, which is a miraculous phenomenon. We need oxygen to breathe, but where does it come from? Look around at all the trees and plant life. They take in carbon dioxide and replace that with oxygen, which is released into the atmosphere through their leaves. Take away all carbon dioxide that is exhaled by all oxygen-breathing animals, and there would be no plant life here on planet Earth. Our planet would be a reflection of the dormant moon. So we breathe in oxygen and breathe out carbon dioxide, and that carbon dioxide gets recycled. This is the cycle, or rebirth, of life.

In considering birth, we need to also consider rebirth. This might be a person having an aha moment or revelation. This important breakthrough might change a person's entire life and outlook. The person may discover religion, discover his or her inner self, or perhaps come to terms with the sense of reincarnation or any number of important discoveries.

Never underestimate the power of birth, for it is happening in every phase of your daily life. Each new day is an opportunity for many types of new birth to occur. Perhaps our pet will have a litter of pups, a mother will have twins, or the sun will rise and give birth to a new day.

The Journey of Wonder

Together we will look at things differently for once in our life to really see.
Let's try and see the wonder in the daily sights around so open and free.
There are many wonders in this world that we see every day.
We dismiss them as common, yet their complexity just blows me away.
Take a pair of mallards just quietly floating in the pool.
The movement of their wings as they are airborne—what a marvelous tool.
The same for the mother bird showing her young how fly away;
They take flight by learning their lesson to repeat it every day.
The many wonders in the world we never give a second thought.
I ask many people what to them is a miracle to be sought.
Most respond with something physical or something to be gained,
Never appreciating the wonders of our Earth—the wind and rain.
Place a seed in the ground; there is a miracle surely to embrace.
Miracles happen every day, yet we dismiss them as commonplace.

Power

The measure of a man is what
he does with power.

—Plato (428 BC-348 BC)

A Storm Is Coming; What Should I do?

One usually thinks of a storm as being weather-related, but it can also be a personal storm. I have experienced many personal storms with my children, because as a parent I feel deeply all the trauma and life challenges they go through. These storms cause anxiety, confusion, pain, fear, and so many other emotions.

But maybe the storm is my own storm. When you work through a problem (storm), if you work hard at it, you become stronger and more content and relaxed. My biggest storm was perhaps my divorce from my husband. That was heart-breaking, and my emotions were all over the place. I needed to work through it, and the best way I found to do this was to sit on the beach on Long Beach Island, stare at the ocean, search my mind for understanding as to why this happened, and move on. I had to come to grips with this new phase of my life and gain perspective on my inner strength.

I am such a believer that our storms make us into better people if we call on that inner strength, listen to the voice in our ears, and thank heavens for our spirit guide, who will help guide us on our new path.

The storm could be a personal spiritual experience. The storm that is coming could also be illness. The storm could also be death looming around the corner. In times when one is in the eye of the storm, one needs to turn to our heavenly Father to help one weather this event. Listen quietly for that still, small voice to guide you through the storm to the other side. It is so important that after you pray you give yourself over to a few minutes of quiet, so that if God is going to speak to you in that still, small voice, you will hear him.

Perception

Everything is moving, everything is in motion, and everything is energy! As the earth rotates and I experience light and darkness, night and day, I have my perception of what it is. But nothing is real, nothing is what I think, and no one sees the same thing. It is not until I learn to silence my mind and allow the true meaning of life and existence to come to me that I will leave my perception behind and be free—free to know more, free to know everything. I am not there yet, but I am on my journey.

This earth is perfect, we are perfect—everything is perfect. But my perception makes me doubt this. Where does this doubt come from? I tell myself I will know one day, and I will. I look around my surroundings and I see (and perceive) perfection all around me. A bird flies, and I know not how and know not why, and yet every winter, he goes south. Who tells him where to go? How does he know which way is south?

I recently watched a movie titled *Salmon Fishing in the Yemen*. Though they were in the desert, they had to make a lake and had to import farm-raised salmon. One day there was a dam break, and the lake was flooded. Everyone thought the Salmon had died, though two days later someone saw a salmon jump. The salmon had swum upstream while the dam water rushed down. They had done what Salmon do. But who taught them? Who told them they would live if they did this? Sometimes I feel like a salmon pushing upstream while everything flows against me, trying to hold me back. I wonder how I find the strength sometimes to move forward, but I do. The next day, my stream flows easier. I wonder, *If I let go of my perception of needing to push forward, will the stream flow easier? Am I pushing too hard and not allowing my life to flow like a river?* How does the saying go— "Water always finds a new path." What does that mean to me?

I believe in my head there is an order for everything. I believe that from the moment I was born, I knew everything, but I do not remember knowing. I have forgotten what I knew. My father once told me something very interesting; he said, "Ask yourself what you knew before you forgot." I know it's still in me; I want to remember.

Today I ask myself, "Show me a different perception in something I would never think, show me something amazing so that I learn and understand more." I hope that when I write again, I will have something amazing to write about because I see and learn something amazing— something I didn't know (or don't remember knowing) before.

Tracy Pendergast
September 9, 2012

Power of the Bible

The power of the Bible lies in the fact that it makes you find your own words and interpretations. There have been hundreds of thousands of copies sold, and the demand gets stronger and stronger each year. Every story within the Bible is told in such a way that it gives you history of an event, and behind each story is a message. It is up to each individual to interpret the meaning of the story or parable. Each interpretation will depend on the past history of the individual and his or her spiritual growth. With the help of our Holy Spirit each person is able to come up with revelations that are unique to him or her.

One can read a passage today and then go back years later and read that same passage and perhaps come up with an entirely different revelation. This is the power of the Bible; it never ceases to instill new thoughts and revelations.

A perfect understanding of the Bible is a never-ending task. Depending on where we are in our journey to heaven, we will view the various stories, the psalms, the Ten Commandments, and the many other messages in a different light each and every time we read this book of knowledge.

The Power of Concept

We all know the story of creation from the book of Genesis, in which God created the earth in six days. He then rested on the seventh day. In this short time frame, God created and finished this process—but in concept only. What does it mean to be created in concept? Concept is an abstract idea—a general notion or a plan of intention. There was no one on earth to see this demonstration of creation, so it was created in concept to be revealed to human eyes when Adam was created to live in this environment.

Another example is the tree, of which there are hundreds of varieties. These trees were created, but they need water and sun to survive; that is the concept or plan created by God. Thus, we have sunshine, rain, and the changing of the seasons. This is a plan that the Lord God created so that in time his children would have a special place to live.

As man evolved, he was able to create, using the power of concept, to build bridges, develop medicine, construct high-rise buildings and bring into existence so many other inventions. Remember the stories of Leonardo da Vinci, born in 1452 who via concept drew pictures of the bicycle, tanks, parachutes, and many other items from various scientific and medical fields. He was also the first to conceptualize flying machines. These pictures flooded his mind, formed out of abstract ideas.

New concepts are there for the conscious mind to create. The Wright Brothers were bike builders, but they had the concept of a bike that would fly. Today we have the airplane, thanks to their early concept of a bike in the sky. Even Henry Ford had a concept of how a horseless carriage should be built, and his conception developed into today's cars.

The unconscious mind brought the concept to the present, and via evolution, many of these early concepts were brought to life.

Concept is a powerful tool that our heavenly Father has given us. We each have a different talent or gift that is unique to self. A songwriter will write down words and notes that come into his or her mind first as a concept, and that concept will then develop into a beautiful song. An artist will have a concept in his or her mind of a picture to be painted and will develop this mental picture into a thing of beauty. We each have a concept of what we would like our life to be like. Thus, this notion or concept is a very powerful force in how we live our daily lives.

What Is Coming?

Today if you ask people where they think this world is headed, you get a lot of very negative answers. The entire world is in such turmoil, and there does not seem to be any letup.

Let's go back to biblical times. Even then the world was in turmoil. The Lord God told Noah to build a huge ark to house two of everything because God was going to cause a great flood to cover the entire planet Earth. God did not want to destroy all living things, but he wanted a new or fresh start, for he was greatly displeased with his people.

But then his people did it again, and we have the story of Sodom and Gomorrah, wherein the Lord God caused the destruction of many cities because of the evil ways of his people. The Bible is full of stories in which God destroyed cities and generations of people because of the debauchery of their ways.

Let's move away from biblical times and see how planet Earth has fared. Mount Vesuvius erupted in AD 79, destroying many cities and killing thousands. In 1815, the major eruption of Mount Pinatubo sent up clouds of ash, changed the climate for months, and destroyed many lives. Even today the news media is full of natural disasters such as earthquakes, floods, fires, and tsunamis, just to mention a few. In nature, we learn, God is a very powerful source. One has to stop and think, "Is the Lord God again displeased with us?" God created our planet, and everything on Earth belongs to him. Is he so displeased with how we, his children, are running our lives here on his creation, that again he is sending up a wake-up call to get us to change our ways?

Are we no different from the people of Sodom and Gomorrah? Look around and you will see greed, sexual immorality, idolatry, conflict, and nations grabbing for more and more power.

All of us have heard of the lost civilizations, the most popular being the city of Atlantis. But what of the Indus Valley in Pakistan some forty-five hundred years ago, the Anasazi settlement in New Mexico of the twelfth century, or, perhaps the oldest, the Clovis culture in New Mexico dating back to eleven thousand five hundred years ago? Many of these civilizations were very advanced in mathematics and engineering. What happened to them? The big question is, What is going to be happening to our present-day civilization?

Looking at the dates of many of these occurrences, we note that God created this planet millions of years ago. His hand has been in its construction and destruction since time began.

What is coming? We, his children here on Earth, have no idea what his ultimate plan for us is. But we do know that in order to arrive in the heavenly world, we as individuals and as a collective whole must change our ways. Regardless of what religion we belong to, God is the Creator of us all. Instead of all the negative emotions, we must begin to express love, kindness, peace, and understanding of each other. "Love your neighbor as yourself. If you keep on biting and devouring each other, watch out or you will be destroyed by each other" (Galatians 5:14–15 NIV).

Let's look at our world today here in the year 2018. Do you think our Lord Jesus would be pleased with how we, the children of God, are taking care of this planet earth that the Lord God prepared for us? Mother Nature has been doing her part to keep our physical planet in good working order. Rains come to feed the soil so it can produce food for animals and for us humans. The sun shines to bring warmth and to help everything to grow and prosper. That takes care of our physical world, but what are we doing to take of our spiritual world?

When the masses converge in one place, miracles and good deeds can indeed happen. When Billy Graham preached in Madison Square Garden, the masses listened and went their separate ways, inspired by the Word of God. When family or friends are facing a crisis, be it regarding health or myriad other issues, we offer up sincere and loving prayers for a good resolution to the problem. God hears these prayers and in his own time will answer the need.

Keep in mind that we are "One nation under God" and that the world we live in today is greatly in need of our constant prayers. The only way to improve this world of today is by positive and constructive use of our freedom of speech—the verbal as well as the nonverbal that springs from within.

Power of Blame

The power of blame
Is always the same.
You look at others
And always choose a brother.
In fact, all troubles are within
That's where the problem begins.
A simple fact is, just control the mind
And you begin to leave it all behind.
Seeing all problems as the same,
Then you are the only one to blame.
Your mind controls all facets of being;
It just takes thought for achieving.
First you need to leave your ego in the dust
So all your past perceptions are then a bust.
Life is perfect; just let the truth flow.
Heaven is here, as sure as the wind does blow.
It works in heaven as on Earth.
We can gain knowledge with every rebirth.

Power of Thought

Our mind is something we should not take lightly.
It has the power of creation, and we should thank heaven nightly.
You may think that the body has all the control,
Yet it is the power of thought and the creation of soul.
Never be confused by the fact you see an outer and an inner;
The truth is they both are the same, and this is a winner.
Being the same means you, as soul, have all the power.
Choosing the inner means you can create perfection by the hour.
We live in a world of opposites, where all have a matching pair.
While in heaven, all are one, no names, so confusion is rare.
Time is always on our mind and is an earthly invention,
Yet in heaven the time is given no attention.

The Power of Water

It rained all day, and it rained all night.
The water was dirty and nasty to the sight.
The streams filled and the rivers overflowed.
The power of the water could not be slowed.
Over roads and yards this mass rushed forward.
Seeping through doors in its path to move onward.
We had no ark to save us from this devastation.
Gather the children; retreat quickly from this situation.
Hurry into the boats as we are surrounded by danger.
Where are the others to save from this water of anger?
Devastation is complete as homes and cars are a loss.
But we have our Lord God to help us bear this cross.
Friends and family open their homes—a safe haven to rest.
With love and prayer, we unite to begin this new quest.
Each day, say a prayer to release your anger and sorrow.
God will be there to lead you forward to a fresh tomorrow.

Louisiana flood—August 2016

Self

This above all: to thine own
self be true.

—William Shakespeare, from *Hamlet* (1600)

Human or Self

We think we are the highest form of life here on earth. We praise ourselves as we move along in time and space, maybe not loving our neighbor but just putting up with him or her. Family is the same; blood may be thicker than water, but if they do not believe the same as each other, conflict is on the horizon.

This is a world of chaos, and all mankind adds to it. Sure, you may not kill or do physical harm to someone, but we all, as self, add a little to the chaos. Do you still think we are the highest thought form?

Think about this. Do fire ants kill other fire ants? Do bluebirds kill other bluebirds? Do jackrabbits kill other jackrabbits? The answer to all is no. Now, do humans kill other humans? The answer is yes, and it has been for hundreds of thousands of years. Why is this, you ask? Because of freedom of thought, we have become so involved in self, and we are separate because of independent thinking. We are always looking for power over others. We forage for money so we can build a bigger house, and then we put locks on all the doors to this house. After that, we build a six-foot wire fence around the whole property.

One might say that if we lived in the wilderness, things would be better, yet if you lived in the wilderness you would have to forage for food, protect yourself from wild animals, and provide basic housing to keep you warm in the winter.

So, do you think the future as we know it is in trouble? This world, according to history, has been reinvented at least seven times; it reverted back to nothing and started over again.

We each make our own happiness and contentment. Spend time each morning with your Holy Spirt. Listen in that quiet time for that small voice in your head. Remember the Golden Rule: "Do unto others as you would have them do unto you." And recall the most powerful words from the Ten Commandments: "Thou shall love thy neighbor as thy self. There is none other commandment greater then these" (Mark 12:31 KJV).

Intelligence

We, as humans, have our own gauge on the intelligence of others, or you may use the slang term "smarts." Intelligence can be more generally described as the ability to perceive information and to retain it as knowledge to be applied toward adaptive behaviors within an environment or context.

The animal kingdom also has its own form of intelligence. The bear perceives that the weather is changing and it is time to hibernate. He knows this from birth, and he retains this knowledge year after year and is well prepared for this long nap.

What of nonmatter and its intelligence? An example would be a tree, which sprouts from a tiny seed and grows to majestic heights. In fall the leaves turn color and fall to the ground; this cycle is completed year after year. Is this considered the intelligence of the tree? The leaves on the ground will then decay and turn into dirt, forming a new cycle of life for worms, bugs, and even nonmatter.

Artificial intelligence is intelligence in machines. It is commonly implemented in computer systems using program software. Robots are being developed that also have artificial intelligence. So, we can conclude that intelligence does take many different forms.

Everything, whether it is human or nonmatter, has its own form of intelligence. It does not depend on what part of this planet the form is located in; it still knows from its own intelligence how to act and conform to the new environment. Another example would be that iron melts at 2,800 degrees Fahrenheit, snow melts above 32 degrees, and water boils at 212 degrees. These are the properties, and the known intelligences, of these products.

Therefore, you have to agree that everything has a role to play.

Everything has a job to do to make this world perfect. One may say these are only rules and not intelligence. Let me ask you this: as a human, do you not have to think to follow our laws when you drive your car, drink a glass of water when your body is thirsty, or lie down when you are tired? When a tree lacks water, it will drop its leaves in order to live another day. How does a tomato seed know it is a tomato and not a cucumber?

Intelligence keeps the cycle of life continuing whether it be human, animal, or nonmatter. What a wonderful gift our Creator has bestowed on us.

Intuition

Intuition is the ability to acquire knowledge without inference or the use of reason. The word "intuition" comes from Latin verb "*intueri*," which is usually translated as "to look inside or to contemplate." Intuition is thus often conceived as a kind of inner perception, sometimes regarded as real lucidity or understanding

We have all experienced a sudden thought or insight of something to do or something that might present itself. This is what we call intuition, and it can be a very strong urge if you listen to your inner self. You might get the sense you should call a friend, only to find out that your friend was going through some very difficult times and your call up lifted his or her spirits. Perhaps your intuition told you to drive a different route, only to find out later that there was an accident on the route you planned.

Intuition can be explained as your spirit guide helping to guide you through your daily life. Therefore, we should all be aware of and listen to that inner voice and act on such thoughts.

Intuition is a very important tool in our freedom of thought, or free will, for it guides us through the maze of our daily lives.

Intuition

Do you ever experience that sense of inner perception?
Does the inner voice guide you in a different direction?
This voice in your ear is your spirit guide leading you forward.
Listen, listen, for it is important to follow this onward.
God has his own plan derived for each of us to follow.
If you are not receptive to this voice, you just may wallow.
Our intuition is that angel sitting on our shoulder, guiding us.
Do not change course or make decisions on merely a guess.
Intuitions are good, for they are that silent guide from above.
Follow your heart as your life unfolds to reveal a life full of love.

Memories

Each and every one of us stores past memories in his or her mind. Memories are nothing more than events that happened in our past, and they are then stored in our minds. Our minds store all these events, which might be sensations, impressions, information, or even just an idea to be recalled when needed. Without memories of our past, we would stagnate and not learn from our past experiences, and thus we would not continue to move forward in this process of learning and growth. The mind is a very sophisticated entity, in that it stores these memories in separate compartments to be called on at a moment's notice, and the mind knows exactly where it stored that memory.

An earthly example would be as follows: You walk into the post office and see one thousand mailboxes on the wall, each with your name listed on the box. Each box is filled with past memories of a thing or emotion. You can open the box and review all these memories from the past. You can build from the good memories and make corrections to overcome the bad memories and learn from that experience. You can then close that box, and all the information will still be available to review or remember at a later time.

Memories are the past, which comes to the present to influence our behavior. It is so important to learn from these memories so that one does not make the same mistake twice. Memories help to form our lives for good or for evil. Memories influence our lives, but it is the Spirit within us that guides us on the path our Lord Jesus Christ wants us to take. Rise above the bad memories and let your spirit soar and rise to the

157

highest heights of what you can become. "But the Comforter, which is the Holy Spirit, whom the Father will send in my name, he shall teach you all things and bring all things to your remembrance, whatsoever I have said unto you" (John 14:26 KJV).

Memories

Our minds are our memory boxes of past events.
Sift through them and learn what each has meant.
We are forever learning how to handle our mistakes.
So let your past be your guide for corrections to make.
Been there, done that; now we must change and move forward.
Our task with Spirit is to correct, improve, and move onward.
Our memories are full of love, patience, and kindness, to name a few.
So begin the process of keeping these emotions alive and new.
The others, like fear, hate, and judgment, will also try to find a place.
Use you past experience so that these emotions will have no space.
Our past memory is our current future, so handle it with pride.
Move forward and grow knowing your spirit guide is at your side.

Mind's Role

The objective mind is the mind we use every day. Conscious of what we see and feel, this is the left side, where we know we know. We experience life here on Earth, and everything is stored as memories. This is the area in which we know we are alive and function in this world. The term "go within" refers to our bubble, where we possess the consciousness and the free will that make our life in the present possible. Through our perception, we create our microcosm. We are all exposed to the universal laws of the land.

The subjective mind, which is on the right side of our bodies, feels the Spirit from within. It follows not man-made laws, but universal law. This is what many would call the higher self. We are aware of our spiritual being within. We are all exposed to the universal laws of the land. These laws are set and exist in wait for our Spirit of the objective self to use them. It is the objective world or the outer self—the external—which will result in an effect.

This subjective mind is the seat of memories of everything that has ever happened to self, lifetime after lifetime. In the Hindu religion, it is the Wheel of Eighty-Four. (According to Hinduism, you have come and gone eight million, four hundred thousand times, changing from mineral to plant, animal, and then human.) In other words, it is your own personal family tree. Under this banner of universal laws, our cities, countries, and races all contain a "family tree" as well. The past is always in play.

Self as Cocreator

When I use the term "self," it really means "Spirit," for self is the physical body, and Spirit is the internal or spiritual being within us.

When we create through the thought process, we create something that has a physical present or matter. But it really is not creating something new; it is just bringing what God created into the present.

Thus, God is the Creator, and man or Spirit is the cocreator

Remember: Genesis states that in six days, all was created. This was in concept only, yet it is very important to remember that it was all perfect; we, as cocreators on the path to perfection, bring in the negative.

Trust me; the heavenly Father never sees this negative aspect of the present.

Self, the Cocreator

There are really two parts to self. There are these bodies of ours that walk the planet. The physical part is what feels emotion, has pain, and creates things via the thought process. The second part of self is the spiritual part, or what we call Spirit. The physical body has no control over the spiritual part of us. But our spiritual part is our guiding light and has great control and influence over this physical body.

Let's take, as an example, an artist. He sits on a mountaintop and wants to paint the glory that surrounds him. But today he is feeling sad, had a fight at home, and is a little depressed. What his eyes see and what he puts down on canvas are quite different. The artist's emotions are tainted by what he sees and feels, and thus the picture is not a true image of what our creator, the Lord God, has established. So, the artist is a cocreator of this scene, as this is not a replica of what God has created.

Now let's say this same artist wakes up early and has a desire to paint a beautiful picture of the landscape from the top of the mountain. Trekking up to the top, he is filled by the wonders of nature. He is listening to that small voice in his head, which is his spirit guide. He sets up his easel and beings to paint the colors and majesty of what is before him. What God created and what he paints are one.

We are cocreators in that we invent things, discover new ways to treat illnesses, and build and develop things. But we do not do these things on our own; our inspiration comes from the still, small voices of our spirit guides. God created this planet, and he has a plan for how he wants things to evolve. We, via our spirit guides, fulfill this greater plan as the cocreator. The inspiration and freedom of thought enable us, with the help of our spirit guides, to design and fulfill the plan that our Lord God has set in motion.

Self's Invincible Power

We, as self, find it hard to believe that we do have power to make things happen and to cause positive change. Therefore, many times we make up things to convince others we do indeed have power. Then we say, "Thank God" or "my Holy Spirit was guiding me." But in truth, did you let our heavenly spirits guide you?

We need to remember that it is via our free will, which was given to us by our heavenly Father, that we, as self, are able to make decisions, develop ideas, and move forward in our onward paths. The big if is this: if we are not in tune with our Holy Spirit and forge out on our own, making a new path, we will never reach perfection and the goal our Father wants us to reach. Yes, we have free will, but behind that stands our Holy Spirit, guiding us, so we must listen to that quiet voice.

It is like when a beloved parent passes on. We cherish many of their thoughts, and their very essence, for these are instilled within us. Often we can feel their very presence and their guidance helping us make decisions. These are angels, which are here to help us on this earthly voyage. Native Americans were very strong believers in the guidance of their ancestors and the guides from the spirit world.

So yes, we, as self, have invincible power. But remember: it is not that we as individuals are so powerful; give credit where credit is due. Our ancestors, our Holy Spirt, and our Lord God are helping us each and every day to fulfill the promise our Father has given to each of us during our time on planet earth.

Sub-Unconscious Myth

My normal time to just sit in quiet for new revelations to come out of the blue is 6:00 a.m. This morning, Spirit was in a hurry, and at 5:58, a voice said, "Drink your coffee later."

That buzzing in your ear that I have talked about for years, you will note, is in the left ear, not the right, which is the unconscious mind.

Here's the truth—and trust me; I could not make this up, for it was news to me at that very moment. The unconscious mind has no ability to create at all. Its job is only to bring the concept to the conscious mind for creation, via what many call the future and what I call the past.

I have said before that in the Bible, Genesis states God created the heavens (Universe) and Earth in six days and rested on the seventh. It makes no mention of him returning on the eighth day to create tomorrow or the next day. This means to me that it was created in totality in concept only, for soul, via free will and perception, created the present daily. So, the unconscious is only bringing us the concept for the conscious mind to create and put cause and effect into play via evolution.

For example, the Wright Brothers were bike builders. They had an idea about a flying machine that could beat gravity. Via evolution we now have the plane. Note that Henry Ford had the same concept, and through his ideas and evolution, we have the car.

Look at Leonardo da Vinci, who in about 1493, he drew a picture of a bike and a computer keyboard. These were concepts that did not become reality until four hundred plus years later.

The older I get, the more I see that this world is made up of simple facts that are just hidden from view until ready. It seems to me that when a new revelation comes to me, it is not new but is just evolution in thoughts that I am asked to share.

The Dream Maker

Whether you are awake or sleeping, you are the dream maker. With every thought you have during the day, you are creating your outside world either in fact or fiction.

Our goal should be eternal truth. While sights and sounds via our thoughts produce outcomes, they may be either true or false in reality. We accept dreams when we are sleeping and try many times to recall them in vain when we awake. Because we are not always successful, we think that it's not us who produced a given dream. Yet during the day, 100 percent of our daily lives are the creation of our thoughts. We think that what is going on around us is out of our control and that some outside source is making this world of chaos. Trust me; this is you, the dream maker, and the laws that make up this place we call Earth, and its main source of power is time.

The world you see, hear, or feel is not on the outside but is within you. The world within is where you will find your Holy Spirit—not the self you think is the body. This Holy Spirit is your guide within and has been your protector; some may call it your higher self.

I keep going back to the power of free will, and we were given this for only one simple reason—so that nothing can affect our lives, freedom, or liberty unless we allow it. If others could control our lives in this time and space, then we would not have been given free will. Stand in the middle of a rainstorm, and you will find yourself wet. With your free will, you open an umbrella over your head, and presto! You are protected. No matrix here.

Time also is your dream maker through your own thinking. Let's say we are sitting on the ocean's shore in the year 1800. We look out to sea and see a ship made of steel a thousand feet long, and some bug-like objects flying off a long, flat deck. We would think we had just seen a miracle or a dream, yet all we did was move to the year 1941. Just to muddy the waters about time, I'll add that I have always said that the time people call the future is really the past coming toward us. The Bible says that God created the heavens and Earth in six days and rested on the seventh. That means it was created in its entirety. And as this past comes into view each day, we, with our free will, create our reality from the concept that God created. How else could Leonardo da Vinci draw the bike and the helicopter, along with a computer keyboard and many other things, hundreds of years before they were invented?

Let's get back on track. Get in touch with that little voice in your head and ask your Holy Spirit to mediate between illusion and truth so that you may gain the knowledge and wisdom within you.

The True Thoughts of Self

The true human goal throughout one's lifetime is to be accepted and liked by others. Every facet of your life is displayed, sometimes subtly and other times in full glory.

Take the actors and actresses of stage and screen, as well as musicians and singers. They all want to be loved, admired, and adored by the public. In order to stay at the top, they must present a certain image to their public, whether or not this is their true self.

The sad part is that via this behavior, we often fail in the real reason we are in the body, which is to love self—the spiritual self, not this material body. If one does not love oneself, one can never expect others to love him or her. When you are happy within, you express a kind and loving aura. Love yourself and others will surely follow suit.

After you roll out of bed, you brush your teeth, comb your hair, put on expensive clothes, climb into your high-end car, and off you go. All for what? The ego can be strong in driving a person to higher and higher expectations just to prove he or she is the best, the richest, or the most talented.

Luckily this applies only to a very small percentage of people, as most strive to be content within themselves, to help and assist others, and to be contributing individuals on this planet Earth. Our time on Earth is very short, so it is important that you do all in your power to leave this planet better off than when you arrived.

The core values of a good person's life are love, faith, honesty, kindness, and integrity. Are these the values you will have left behind for others to reap the benefits from?

Universal Mind

Universal mind exists only in the outer self. It is the center of intelligence. Every time you think, it sets in motion an action and then a creation. Remember: free will is within the outer self or the conscious mind. Therefore, on the outer self we are able to recruit other souls to complete the task.

Because of the oneness of the mind (it is the same mind for us all), the mind cannot contradict any thought given. Christ knew this: This is proof that if one word has power, so the law is. All words have power, so choose your speech with care.

Universal laws do not choose ever. They are set laws. For example, take electricity; it can be used to heat your house or cook your dinner.

Leading to the answer that we are all one, think of it that way. God is our creator. He is the Father and created us all in his image and likeness—not one smarter than another, but all the same.

So then, how could we not be one with one another, for we are of the same cloth? Here is a simple example: A tree grows in size and splendor, but would one say its branches and leaves are not part of the tree? In its totality, it is all one!

If we, as soul, are not one with others, then how can we be one with God? We were given free will for only one reason—not to be separate, but to be in control of our thoughts. So, on our own, we should learn, love, and be a part of God as one.

I believe 100 percent of the people who don't understand this concept aren't able to understand it because they would then lose the power of thought, which makes up self. When you join all other selves, this is perfection with God, the power of many, and the joining of all and reconnecting perfectly in God.

Know this: the heavenly Father sees us in secret; we don't see him, yet we must believe he is there.

In closing, I offer the riddle of the apparent separation between God and man. What makes self think it is not one? You must know that we are all eternal beings and are given not only free will but also the power of thought to dream of the unknown. We work daily to move ahead, moving to the divine center, knowing that upon acceptance of oneness with all beings and the return to the Source of Creation, love will overwhelm you as you enter the gates of eternity. Self is one, and one is self!

Universal Mind

It has been my understanding that we are connected in thought.
This makes me uncomfortable, for there are many that are badly taught.
To be connected to a murderer or bomber is depressing.
This is not how it works, as I lay out step-by-step by regressing.
Know that mind is consciousness, not a thing.
There two mindsets, sub objective and objective, to bring.
Subjective self goes within, where free will controls.
Objective, the outer universe, is where the Creator patrols.
We, then, are not connected in the bubble of self's subjective inner,
but the objective outer, where perfection is the winner.
So we are all together when ego is acknowledged for rejection.
The soul moves to the objective to join the Creator's world of perfection.

How Did We Come to Be

How did we come to be?
Let's start with the oak tree.
Years ago, it was only four feet tall.
Over the years, it just grew and grew; that's all.
A simple tomato will grow from a variety of cells.
Then it dies and leaves behind lots of seeds; oh well.
The evolution will develop many new and different seeds,
So now we have various tomatoes to satisfy our many needs.
The horse and buggy is another interesting evolution.
Thanks to Ford and others, we have the auto solution.
The big question is, How did we come to be?
We have evolved and developed to be a person like me.

Power of Self

The bird that sails by you has not been told it can fly.
So why are we so restricted to what we can do on high?
Reach down within yourself, and let this light guide the path.
The heavens will open, and the next step will enlighten at last.
See our glory develop through this vibration from above.
Nothing is stronger than our belief in heavenly love.

Soul

What keeps life fascinating is the
constant creativity of the soul.

—Deepak Chopra
(1947 -)

Light Is the Energy of Soul

Light is the energy of soul; nothing exists that is not present by way of light. When you view something with earthly eyes, you are looking at what science calls nonmatter in the form of light.

Let me give you an earthly example: A producer creates a movie; it appears in a theater, and one hundred people enter and sit in the seats to watch this production. Keep in mind that the film that appears, which seems to be complete in scope, is really only the concept of the director's thoughts and his direction. Each of the one hundred people who came to view this film will fill in the blanks in accordance with his or her past history and his or her own interpretation. So, the movie may make you laugh or cry; some will like it, while others may not. This is all because of our past history and how we view and interpret things. Now, after two hours, up comes "The End." What happens next? One hundred leave their seats, and another one hundred come in and take those empty seats for another showing. Then the same identical film is shown to all those different people, each of whom is left with a different impression of the same material.

One might say we live in a repeat world because everything repeats, such as the movie in the example above. Every new day is a repeat; you get up and go to work or to school, your daily routine is a repeat of eating, driving, sleeping, and so on. I hope this repeat sequence includes time to reflect with your spirit guide and your inner soul. One could also say life is a habit of things we do and say. Be sure that the inner light of your soul is expressed in everything you do each day.

Light is the energy of soul; the heavenly light from above shines down on us, directly into our very souls. This light, along with our spirit guides, is the energy we need to perform the many tasks required of us each day. Some of our tasks are in the material world, but so many are of a spiritual nature. We all have heard that voice in our head guiding us to make certain decisions or to take a certain path. This is not a mistake to be overlooked. Do not think for a minute that this is your thought process; give credit where credit is truly due.

Light has tremendous energy, and it imparts this energy into each and every one of us. It is what makes a scientist able to come up with new complex theories, gives the artist or musician the power of creativity, and gives a mother the strength and energy to raise her children.

Soul Is the Light

The miracle of light we see on earth with our eyes—
It's a simple story of how without our knowledge, we are wise.
We see a tree fall at a distance of a mile or two,
Yet we hear the sound of the fall moments after our view.
What our eyes see arrives at the speed of light,
While the sound is much slower and arrives later in spite.
This tells me my eyes view only light in everything I see.
So what is its source? For all objects are the same to me.
The answer then lies in that all objects are made up by souls.
They are unconscious in nature, yet a purpose to unfold.
Souls have always been the source of light.
I thank you for the wisdom to get this puzzle right.

We Are Soul

A few days ago, my friend Micki sent me this phrase:

> You do not have a Soul
> You are a Soul
> Yet
> You have a body

Today this got me to thinking. We each have a body with a different name for self so we can feel different. When we build a home, the first thing we do is build a fence so everyone knows that this is our house. Deep down, we believe we are only self, while the Bible states, "I and my Father are One" (John 10:30 NIV).

Look in the mirror, and what do you see with the eyes that are in this body of yours? Do you see your soul, or do you only see your physical body? Why, then, are we not seeing the light of soul? The reason is that we truly think we *are* the body and not that we *have* a body.

How do we start to see soul in the mirror instead of the face of this physical body? It's a lot easier than one thinks and can be done in thirty days. I would guess you look into a mirror ten or fifteen times a day. Another twenty times a day, you are looking, thinking, or doing something with this body of yours. You look in the mirror while brushing your teeth, combing your hair, putting on makeup, or shaving. How about when you are passing a mirror in the hall? Do you take a quick glance?

There are even more actions that take place daily with this body of yours: selecting which outfit to wear, choosing shoes and socks, and getting your nails trimmed. How about taking a nice, long warm shower and washing your hair? When breakfast is done, along with all the actions required to accomplish that feat, you then go to work, take a walk, or head to the gym. This is your body in action every minute of the day.

What I am asking you to do here is stop and focus on words and thoughts. Focus on these rather on what you are doing, for this is soul; you are not a body, but you are soul. Remember also that when you are feeling sick, it is not soul that is sick; it is your mind trying to fool you. The Bible states over and over, "Be ye therefore perfect, even as your Father which is in heaven is perfect" (Matthew 5:48 KJV).

I have been saying for years that the body is the carrier for soul, but the body takes orders via the mind. Remember what I said about that buzzing in your ear, which is your life source from the heavenly world. When the body no longer has that connection, the body stops all action or function. And the next thing you know, dirt is being thrown over your body. I guess what I am saying is that everything you do for the body is material; do not be fooled into thinking it is spiritual!

Here is a great earthly example: You build a house for yourself, for you are tired of living as a cave dweller. You build a nice one-story house, put on siding and paint it a pleasant color, and add a nice roof and pretty windows as well. Next you landscape the outside with trees and shrubs, a sod lawn, and, of course, a garden with lots of flowers. Why did you do all of this? The answer is simple; you wanted to make the house look its best in your material world.

We have to focus on soul, not the material body. First ask your inner spirit guide for help. Secondly, do your part every day. Know you are soul so that the Spiritual world knows you mean what you have asked for. Old habits take time to change, so leave notes everywhere to remind soul and body that things are changing. This is the secret for success.

I have a phrase I state over and over each day. Some of you just starting along this path should put reminders on mirrors, next to your computer, or on your refrigerator. My statement comes from Genesis: 1:27: (KJV) "So God created mankind in his own image." It is also stated in Genesis 9:6 (KJV) as "for in the image of God made he man."

"The best love is the kind that awakens the Soul and makes us reach for more, that plants a fire in our hearts and brings peace to our minds. And that's what you've given me. That's what I'd hoped to give you forever" (Nicholas Sparks).

Mirror, Mirror on the Wall

Mirror, mirror on the wall, I can't see my inner self at all.
Am I somewhere hidden behind that reflection in this wall?
Like everyone, I have a body created just for me.
I am the same but different, as everyone can see.
This body has a name, which makes me different from the rest.
On the material side, I am made up of blood, bone, and flesh.
There is also a spiritual side of this body in which I reside.
That special present is the soul, who is my light and guide.
This material body will decay, die, but my soul will live into eternity.
My soul will return from whence it came; I know this with such clarity.
Mirror, mirror on the wall, now I can see my inner self just fine.
The soul deep inside wants to make me a person of light to shine.
Yes, I have a body, but I must know that a soul I do possess.
The great "I Am" made me, thus I am soul, for I have been blessed.

What Is Soul?

Religions and philosophers over the centuries have tried to come up with the meaning and definition of the word "soul." One definition is "The spiritual or immaterial part of a human being or animal, regarded as immortal." Do you find it interesting that the soul is also mentioned as part of the animal kingdom?

Here is another definition from Merriam-Webster: "the spiritual part of a person that is believed to give life to the body and in many religions is believed to live forever." Interesting to note is that it states, "give life to the body." Does that mean that if you do not have soul, there is no life to the body? Along these same lines, the ancient Greeks also believed the soul was that which gave the body life. It was considered spiritual, as in the breath that gives life.

Socrates said that even after death, the soul exists and is able to think. Many who believe in reincarnation believe that when the body dies, the soul continues on through rebirth in a new body.

I remember hearing the story of a family in the hospital with a loving member close to death. As they all were around, praying and comforting each other, the nurse came in and went to the window and opened it. She told the family that their loved one was close to death and she wanted to let his soul soar and be free.

As stated by Micki, you do not have a soul, for you *are* soul, yet you do have a body. Yes, we do have a body, and it is within that body that the soul, which is us, resides. The body is flesh and blood and is disposable, yet the soul is the essence of you and will go on for eternity.

Let's look at the many ways the word "soul" is used:

- If you have done an unkind thing against someone, or you have broken a commandment, you cannot escape the guilt in the inner recesses of your soul.
- "Bless your soul" is a common remark.
- "Poor soul" is a term used for an unfortunate being.
- It is used to indicate individuals, as in the line "That town has barely any souls living there."

There are many examples where "soul" is mentioned in the Bible:

"… while the ark was a preparing, where in few, that is, eight souls were saved by water." (1 Peter 3:20 KJV)

"And the Lord God formed man of the dust of the ground, and breathed into his nostrils the breath of life; and man, became a living soul." (Genesis 2:7 KJV)

As stated on Wikipedia, "God did not make a body and put a soul into it like a letter into an envelope of dust; rather he formed man's body from the dust; then, by breathing divine breath into it, he made the body of dust live."

My own interpretation of soul is that it is my inner most core—the essence that makes me who I am today. I believe that my spirit guide and my soul are related and work together to help me manage this earthly plane. I cannot have one without the other. At my time of death, both of these entities will move on and I will have a rebirth. Mother said to me shortly before she died that she could not and would not believe that this life was all there was. She did not believe she had gained so much knowledge just for it to die with the death of her physical body.

My soul was reborn on the day of my birth in 1935. This same soul is working daily with me to make the choices in life that I make. My soul is what keeps me close to God on a daily basis. I like to think that Mother's, Dad's, and Bart's souls are still out there, looking down on me. I read once that our souls reunite with those in our family who have passed on. I think we all want to believe that upon death we will see our loved ones again, though certainly not with the physical body that will be left here on Earth to be returned to dust. Our souls will soar, and we will indeed be reunited, and perhaps we will return again to Earth in a more advanced and higher form. Who knows? That is the mystery of life!

Spirit

For God didn't give us a spirit of timidity,
but a spirit of power, of love and
self-discipline.

—Timothy 2:7 (NIV)

Creation Spirit

There is not one drop more or one drop less of water on Earth now than there was when Earth formed billions of years ago. Earth is enclosed, meaning nothing can move in and nothing can move out. It is as it was created by God.

Souls are exactly the same. When we say, "We are all one," that refers to souls' past, present, and future; for we don't realize it, but the earth is living in the now. As stated in the Lord's Prayer, offered by Jesus Christ on the Sermon on the Mount, "Thy Kingdom come. Thy will be done in earth, as *it is* in heaven." (Matthew 6:10 KJV). The story in Genesis, Chapter 1 states that this Earth was a completed creation and accomplished in only six days. It is only our perception that makes it seem different. Resting occurred on the seventh day not because God was tired; the seventh day is the now, when perfection exists. God created the concept of the future, and it is we who need only to discover and to understand how it was created.

What we need to do as humans is look beyond what we see with our eyes. The eyes don't see; it is the mind that creates the image first, and then the eyes see. The big step for everyone is to stop and go to his or her inner world and ask for a revelation via his or her spirit guide to show him or her a simple truth. If you change your inner thoughts and perceptions, then the outer self has to follow. You will find that daily, while you sit in a quiet place, new answers will come and things will, to your amazement, make better sense. It takes a little practice to guide the mind. You never can shut it down, for the law is that it works twenty-four hours a day, seven days a week, but you can get it on your side.

Discovery is in our nature; we just have to know how to tap this resource. These intelligent laws are meant to be used. Just ask for knowledge and guidance. That is why we have these spirit guides within. They are just waiting for you to wake them up. Throughout your whole life, they have been helping you, so bring them to the forefront now.

Holy Instant

The holy instant is about leaving time behind in the objective (outer) world and entering the now. The world we see is controlled by time and space, with all its pitfalls of life. A holy instant is when we choose the Holy Spirit instead of our ego as our leader.

If you want a healing or a correction of a problem, it will never be resolved in the outer world but must come from within. Let's look at healing; you may ask a dozen questions to try to determine what is wrong. But these are negative questions concerning how bad you feel or how large your problem is.

The now is something different. It is the next step higher than the present, which we all try to stay in. It's hard, for time pulls us into the past and future. The past is history, and the future we don't have a clue about.

Christ walked in the now 100 percent of the time, while the outer world marched to its own drummer. You need to understand the now; it is perfect and changeless. That is how Christ healed the sick and fed the thousands with just six fishes and five loaves of bread, for as one was taken, another one took its place, until in the end they had bushels of leftover food.

So, when you can, sit in quiet and move into this zone with God and Christ where healing is not yet completed. God created man in his image and likeness, which was perfect. The illusion of the past, present, and future, along with time, is corrected in the mind.

Again, a holy instant is the instant in which you are connected to our heavenly Father. The one you want it to be, it is. In other words, every instant is an opportunity, so choose wisely. Make it holy!

The moment this magnitude of spiritual thoughts dawns on you,

you acknowledge it to self. God's plan is the only plan; yours is of the ego or self. It is this holy instant that corrects our misperceptions and alien thoughts. Gladly give over all your plans to the heavenly Father, for this is true reality—not the false belief of the ego!

What my Holy Spirit is telling me at this holy instant is this: The ego tries to rule here in the world of matter. All your plans and dreams ought to serve only self, via our free will, not trying to change others. It is only when you acknowledge this as truth that you are able to drop all your plans and accept that which is shown to you in the instant of time and make it a holy instant.

I will gladly turn over my plans, where each second is spent in service to God and it is his plan, not mine. During holy instants, we take stock of our lives, realize we must forgive, and release misperceptions in our path to a truly enlightened presence.

The hardest thing to comprehend is that Earth is in ego's control, while God is present only via our faith and thoughts. God, however, created Earth in concept only and in perfection. It is important to know that the ego has no creative power, but it does a good job of messing with our thoughts, which can be creative, and then showing negative reality as false.

In time, we the people come to the light. God could not be present here, for God sees only perfection, but there is a master plan of good. We learn that only perfection will lead us home. We then enter the holy instant, which is our way home.

You have to understand this: Earth, in concept, was created perfect. Ego has no power to create, so it is all on us. Most important is that ego is here only by the approval of God so we may learn perfection via our free will. This builds us into true faith that when we return home we are one and we have earned it.

When Spirits Speaks

Of course, Spirit is with us every minute of every day. Whether we are in the house, on the road to work, or just sitting outside in the sun, our Spirit Guide is always with us. Many times, we are open to our Spirit and follow the silent directions, and we have a very good outcome. But there are other times when we are so busy with the material world that we do not hear the warnings from our spirit guides.

Today I am writing about the quiet times when you are sitting in a chair at home, maybe in meditation or just in a quiet space. You are looking for an answer to a situation that is not going well or just some guidance to bring you to a happy solution. How do you know that Spirit is talking to you or if this voice in your head is coming from another source? The problem, more times than not, is that you have been looking to correct this situation on your own and a form of solution. You may think you are asking Spirit for guidance, but if you are headstrong and feel you know what steps to take, then you are not open to the voice and words of the Holy Spirit. The thoughts in your head will be only your thoughts.

When you address Spirit and ask for guidance, you have to clear your own mind of preconceived ideas of how you think things should go. Stop with you own ideas and sincerely say, "I need your help!" When the thoughts come through, they are new and on target and are the answers for correction of the situation. You may say to yourself, "Why did I not think of this before?" You know the reason, for there are millions of ideas in the atmosphere and you have allowed them to enter your private space.

Let me share how over the years Spirit has opened the door to hundreds of subjects that I could never dream up on my own. Because

I believe 100 percent in my source, no matter how hard it is for me to believe, I know it's the truth. I do now ask for earthly examples so that when I am directed to share these thoughts with others, they are easier to understand. Spirit tells me many times that others may not except these as truth now, but in time the door will also open for them. Many souls today are so connected to the material world that it takes time to expand thought to the unseen. This is okay, for we are all on the same journey and time is not a factor.

The Bible is a perfect example. Each story is written so that, depending on your spiritual development, the truths behind the written word expose themselves in different ways to each reader. There is no other writing in this world that can do this.

The story of creation, with Adam and Eve, Cain and Abel, and Noah and the ark, all have deeper meaning than just the written words. Every story and parable in the Bible has a message, and each individual will have his or her own interpretation of the meaning, depending on where he or she is in his or her life journey.

Spirit has given me an unbelievable ride in this life journey I am on. During my meditation, I have gone back in time several times to see other planes, a view of the heavenly lights, and the trillions of souls on their journey of development on this miracle we call earth. I did ask my spirit guide why I am unable to visit what many call the future but I call the past. The answer was very simple: "The space is only a concept." This means that as it moves to the present via the soul's free will, it is created from moment to moment. As an example, again take Leonardo da Vinci, who in about 1542 drew a picture of a bike, a helicopter, and a keyboard, though he had no idea what they were, for they were conceptual only. It took some four hundred years to move them into the present for creation and development.

You know Spirit is speaking when the idea is new. Listen and follow what you have heard; never be afraid to move forward.

Where Has Spirit Gone?

Have you ever had the feeling that you have lost the presence of your spirit guide? There can be any number of reasons why you feel you are alone. Is your life so crammed full of stuff and activities that you have not had a quiet time to focus on your spiritual side?

Our Holy Spirit is with us always, and you only have to ask, pray, or listen for his wise thoughts to flow through your system. Remember: The Holy Trinity is the Father, Son, and Holy Ghost. They are there to guide our daily lives and to keep us on the path our Creator has set out for us.

Richard Warren wrote in his book *The Purpose Driven Life* that "life on earth is a test. An important test is how you act or feel when you can't feel God's presence in your life. Sometimes God intentionally draws back and we do not sense his closeness."

There are many examples of this test in the Bible. Perhaps the most noteworthy one is the book of Job. Poor Job lost everything: his land, his children, and even his wealth. It would appear that the Holy Spirit had left him, but Job never doubted. In time, all was restored to him. King David is another example of feeling the loss of the Holy Spirit. While nailed to the cross, Jesus Christ called out to his father, "… My God, my God, why hast thou forsaken me? (Matthew: 27:46 KJV).

At a critical point in your life, the Holy Spirit may withdraw from you to test your character. How you respond to this challenge is paramount in your development along your spiritual path. Will you step up to the plate with strength, compassion, and faith, or will you be weak and ineffective? If you understand that life is a test, you will then know that nothing is insignificant in your life, and you will be able to move forward.

After a period of absence, I feel that my footprints in the sand today lie beside another set. Tomorrow there will be one set, as Spirit will know that I am sorry for my past thoughts and that I miss the Holy Father with all my heart. There will be one set of prints as Spirit carries me back to the heavenly world of thought.

Footprints in the Sand

Years ago, I read a short paper on footprints in the sand.
It was about one's Spirit and how enlightenment began.
It started out as one walked along the sandy shores.
She sometimes felt so all alone, yet her hope was restored.
Her words were "When I looked behind me, there were two sets that appeared,
Yet during hard times, to my surprise, only one set," and that brought her to tears.
At this interval in time, Spirit informed her it was heaven's design.
"A single footprint in the sand was when I carried you through hard times."
The moral of this story is that we are never alone,
For the task of your Holy Spirit is to show you the path home.
Praise the heavenly Father for the lessons we learn in earthly form.
When falsehoods turn to perfection, we then are heavenly born.

Spirit Leading Me

Spirit, you are leading me to express in words the world I see,
Yet on a personal level, I feel you are leaving me.
I ask for personal guidance, and the answer never flows.
Yet I know you are near, even when no answers show.
I am always asking you to show me the light.
While I know you are present, all I ever seem to see is the night.
I ask you to please take control of my life and show me the now.
I just sit in quiet, waiting, waiting, not knowing how.
I must not be ready and should trust the above,
For I have such deep feeling and feel Spirit's love.
When the time is right,
I will see the light,
For the heavenly world acts with such perfection.
Prayers answered with no rejections.
We are here to accept and to show no concern.
In time the answer will come when it is our turn.
For my goal is to channel heaven here on Earth
To lead us, each and every one, to our own rebirth.

Time

A man who dares to waste one hour
of time has not discovered the value of life.

—Charles Darwin (1809-1882)

Future Being Revealed by the Past

I have said and written dozens of times that the future is really the past coming toward the present. This I believe because in about the 1470s Leonardo da Vinci drew the bicycle, helicopter, and a computer screen with a keyboard in the foreground. This is a prime example of the future being revealed in the past.

For years I have stated this world is 100 percent illusion, created by our own perception. Because of our own free will, each soul (including you and I), creates its own world of illusions. To confirm this truth, if what you and I see with our own eyes were true reality, then we would all see objects exactly the same. Yet we don't, for we each see thing differently because of our past history.

For example, a farmer with many generations of farming behind him would look at a field of wheat with a great sense of satisfaction for a crop well grown and ready for harvest. But a salesman driving down the road might see a field of wheat and think, "Boy, is this land barren." How about the builder who sees this same field and thinks, "I could build such a great housing development on this land"? Perception or illusion, call it what you will. Because of our past history and events that influenced our lives, we see each thing differently.

What we have done here on Earth is put illusion before truth, which is okay; this is how we grow. Remember that we have taken that simple hut made of sticks and stones and now turned it into a large two-story house; this is what we call "evolution." If we all looked at the same old weeping willow tree, which is in reality tall, strong, and leaning to the right, our perception, or illusion, of this tree might be one of beauty or grace and life, or perhaps, because it is leaning, one of death, as it is likely to soon be turned into firewood.

Genesis states that in six days, the heavens and Earth were created. The complexity of this world to date is unbelievable, and just think how complex it will become in the next billion years. The conclusion is simple; God created it in concept only. This is similar to the hut created by primitive man that evolved into a larger two-story house; this was done through man's perception of what could be. A concept of the horseless carriage became the Ford Model T, and the evolution of the motor vehicle came about through man's perception. Take the primitive men who designed the wheel; this changed history, as no longer did man have to carry goods; this is an example of the past coming to the future via development.

Universal laws, along with God's creations, are always perfect, and neither has a right or wrong outlook; therefore, it is the perception of man that creates chaos. Trillions of souls will pass through this place we call Earth on their way to perfection. What I am saying is that there are billions behind us waiting to enter the stream forward. I have used the example of a theater. A hundred souls enter the theater and sit down to view a movie on the screen. Each sees the same image on screen, yet each, due to individual past history, has a different feeling. Some will laugh, while others will cry. When the movie is over and they all exit the theater, the movie is not discarded, for another hundred souls will enter to view this film. In our past, the same things happen as well.

Know this also: all my revelations come via my spirit guide. I know that I personally have very little knowledge of the Bible, yet I am always led to passages that confirm these thoughts. I also know that our entire history, from start to finish, is somewhere in that book. This writing is meant for every living soul, for no matter where you are on the spiritual path, this book has meaning and is meant to start you thinking. The phrase "Living Water and rebirth" has great meaning to me today as compared to a year ago, for our spirit guides take us on this journey of evolution slowly.

Looking back billions of years ago, It is plain to see that creation was very simple. Then, in preparation for mankind and upon his arrival, it also was very simple; there were caves to live in, and the landscape was very simple. Just sit and think for a second at how it is today, and this is nothing compared to how it will be in another five hundred years from now.

A lot of things are in play: God the Creator, man the cocreator, universal mind, and the oneness of soul with the power of free will. People often ask, "Why am I here?" To start with, you have to understand what here really is. It is a state of mind, not a place, for as I have said, Earth is an illusion, and if it were a reality, we would see and experience the same thing, but we don't, because we are in a different location on our path to spiritual development.

This is the reason we have time and space—so we feel that we are moving along. With each new day, we are able to change and grow in knowledge and wisdom on the road to return our perception and self to the oneness of heaven. For in reality, we have never left the place we call heaven. You will note as you look around you that everything is always in the flux of change. Nothing ever stays the same; all material things are in a state of decay, obsolesce, and change, no matter how we try to preserve them. This is the law of this place we call Earth. Change is a good thing, for it gives us the opportunity to reach perfection and a path to our true home in heaven with our Lord God.

How Are Space and Time Related on Earth?

Relativity in physics is a theory developed by Albert Einstein that says the way anything except light moves through time and space depends on the position and movement of someone who is watching. How are space and time related on Earth, and what role do both play in the heavenly world?

When a new living soul is conceived, there are elements of time and space both physical and spiritual involved. How can this cell no bigger than the size of a pinpoint develop into a six- or nine-pound baby with hands, feet, eyes, nose, and ears all in the proper place? The time frame is nine months from conception to birth; that is physical time. This tiny embryo in located in a very small, tight space within the womb. This space will grow and expand to accommodate this new living soul. This space is a physical space. But what happens during this entire process exists within the spiritual realm. Remember: God, our heavenly Father, is the one who created man. Each new living soul is a creation from the heavenly Father. Who determined the time frame for birth if not the heavenly Father? Who made the woman's body able to conceive the new living soul and to expand to provide enough space for this growing infant?

The time this new living soul will have on Earth is very short in the scheme of things. Considering Earth is billions of years old, the human lifetime is but a blip in time. What is important to consider is the time frame for us once we leave this earthly place. Has this being been on Earth centuries before and is now being reborn as a new living soul in a new era? What space did this living soul occupy on Earth now or before?

202

The new mother of this new living soul sees this infant living in her space, breathing air in her home. She watches time mature her child. But then the mother of a child who may have lived two thousand years ago sees her child breathe air in her home and grow old in her lifetime. Time and space are relative to who is watching!

As stated by a pastor, "The Spirit is totally in the spiritual realm and the soul appears to be formed in the processing of combining the Spirit with the physical being."

Many of us wear wristwatches that tell us the time here on Earth, but what is God's time? Years ago, our expected time on Earth was perhaps forty to fifty years, but today it is over eighty or ninety years. In the future, will living souls live to be 120 years old or even longer? Doesn't it make you wonder what God's timetable is for Earth and its inhabitants?

Have you ever heard someone say, "I need my space"? What does that really mean? Here on Earth, "space" could mean time alone in the mountains or on the plains in wide-open space. But it could also mean space for your mind to be quiet and reflect. The mind needs nourishment like the body needs food. We need to let our minds run free so we can have all the emotions of love, peace, patience, and forgiveness, as well as all the other God-given graces available to us.

On a dark night, looking up at the sky, you can see thousands of little bright dots. What are these dots, and what do they contain? This is our universe; if nothing else, it is space! We have orbited the Earth and looked down on our planet from above. But that which is above is so vast and is impossible to conceive. But I guess the way anything moves through time and space depends on the position and movement of someone who is watching. Is that you?

Interval of Time

Let me make a point here regarding past, present, and future. They are all controlled by time, yet time is man-made. Take an apple, for example; in every city in the world, it is an apple. But time may be different from one city to the next around the world, depending on the location of that city on this planet.

Another example is that in the spring, we move the clocks forward, and when we are tired of that, in the fall, we move them back. When you are having fun, time just seems to fly by, yet put you in the dentist chair or waiting room at a doctor's appointment, and it almost stops.

In the heavenly world, the now is timeless, for without time, everything stays the same.

Interval of Time

The totality of all the yesterday's makes us what we are today.

We can't change the past, but it helps us to continue without delay.

If you dwell on the present interval of time, the old can never become new.

The past has value, for it challenges you to see this life through.

Past memories may have a history of being perceived as good and bad,

So you may restrict your adult development, and that is sad.

Letting the past fade is a simple way of moving forward and leaving the rest behind.

When you are young, you are creating your now at every moment in time,

So you just need to have faith in your spirit; trust that all will be fine.

As you age, you must allow the future to unfold to the now with ease.

Then come to the realization that the future is an opportunity to seize.

You will realize that the future is really the past; and you say, "How can this be?"

Our perception creates our present; this you will come to see.

Life Is a Journey

Life is a journey that can be both sadness and fun.
We have different lifetimes; in reality, it is only one.
Years and years of history go by in a flash.
Time is only to show a start; that's its only task.
While this trip through evolution may seem complex at best,
It is only the starting point, and we are given many a test,
Looking ahead to experience so much in Earth years.
Yet there is a plan set in place and nothing to fear.
You may say, "What is the benefit, for it seems like a waste of time?"
Are you telling me you have a better plan in mind?
Honestly, I have seen self's work here on Earth.
I think I will stick with God's plan and wait for another rebirth.

Time Is a Gift

For some people, time has a start and a finish, as in a race. You start, you finish, and what is your time? These people are racing against time. Many in their daily lives feel they are racing against the clock to get to work, pick up the kids, complete assignments, and perform many other tasks.

Each of us wakes up each morning and is given twenty-four hours of time for that day. We cannot add an extra hour to the day; nor can we delete one hour. It is a fixed time, and everyone gets the same allotment, regardless of whether he or she is a productive person or someone who likes to lie around and sleep. It is up to you how you will use the hours of each day. Will you squander them and have nothing to show for it at the end of the day, or will you do something constructive with this gift given to you each and every day? When you awake tomorrow, you will get the same allotment of time as the day before, with nothing added and nothing reduced.

Have you ever been working on a project and said, "I wish I just had another hour"? Time does not work that way. You get twenty-four hours to complete your tasks for that day. There is no carryover, so you might have to use time from your following day's allotment to complete your project. So, remember: time is a gift to each and every one of us; it is guaranteed to be given to you at twelve o'clock midnight—a new and fresh start of a new day.

> To every thing there is a season, and a time to every purpose under the heaven: A time to be born, and a time to die; a time to plant, and a time to pluck up that which is planted; A time to kill, and a time to heal; a time to

break down, and a time to build up; A time to weep, and a time to laugh; a time to mourn, and a time to dance; A time to cast away stones, and a time to gather stones together; a time to embrace, and a time to refrain from embracing; A time to get, and a time to lose; a time to keep, and a time to cast away; A time to rend, and a time to sew; a time to keep silence, and a time to speak; A time to love, and a time to hate; a time of war, and a time of peace. (Ecclesiastes 3:1–8 KJV)

Praise the heavenly Father that in heaven there is no time; there is just eternity, or infinity, for everything there just is!

Time Is Still

As humans in bodies here on Earth, time is always on our minds. Sunrise, sunset, go to work, drive home, and on and on it goes. Are ten years a lot, or fifty years, or even one hundred years more?

Hindus believe in the Wheel of Eighty-Four, which refers to the eight million four hundred thousand reincarnations the normal human goes through in different forms on the path to enlightenment before he or she returns to heaven. In my opinion, that number might be one hundred or even a thousand times more, since our planet earth is thirteen billion years old, and possibly five billion years older than that, give or take another billion.

I know that trillions of souls have already moved from the perception of Earth to be returned to the heavenly world. Why is this speculation important? Knowledge and wisdom are our ticket off Earth. When we understand time, it no longer will control our lives. The fact is that time exists only here, for heaven is eternal.

I have said many times before, "Anything you can't take with you from here on Earth must then be an illusion." Old age and time are one and the same—an illusion. On Earth, both have a purpose—the delineation of the start and end of all events. This is so we can move on to another lesson during the process of reincarnation.

Nothing here is without reason. Truth is never the agreement or argument; it is the interpretation that always brings an opposite into the fold.

What Is Our Future to Be?

Each and every one of us is a child of God. He knew us even before we were conceived. We trust in the Lord, and we know in our heart of hearts that he does have a plan for us. He knew long before we were born what our future would hold. Now it is up to each of us to discover what that path is and to follow it.

As a child, we are so dependent on our earthly parents to guide, nurture, and provide for us. These earthy parents shape and mold us into the people we are to become. That is well and good for the children that have parents who love them, teach them by example, and instill in them all the right virtues and values necessary to advance in this life. But what about those parents who do not want the job of parenting and find a child to be a burden and a chore? What is the future for their children?

Here again God has a plan for all children, regardless of what their home life might have been like. We have often heard of an underprivileged individual rising above his or her surroundings to be become a figure of great respect, perhaps famous in a particular field. Do you think for one minute that just happens by chance as a fluke or a lucky break?

Take, for example, three children raised in the same family with the same upbringing who all turn out differently and lead very different lives. Again, the universal path is at work.

Let me address the concept of "What is our future to be?" Mary Jane wants to be a model, to be famous, to be on the cover of *Vogue* magazine, and to make lots of money. She works hard, goes from agency to agency, watches her diet, and socializes with the right people. The problem is that Mary Jane is only five foot five and thus too short to be a model. No matter how hard she tries to break into this field, she will never succeed. Brokenhearted, Mary Jane returns to her parents' home to reevaluate her life goals. Modeling was not what God had in mind for Mary Jane. He wanted her to be a model of a different sort. Perhaps his plan was for her to be a model teacher, a model missionary, or even just a model parent.

All of us go through many different stages in our development. As babies, we are dependent; as toddlers, we are inquisitive; as teenagers, we are exploratory; as young adults, we live through experience. Then we go from mature adults into old age. Each of these steps shapes and molds us into the individuals we will become.

What are the traits and values that will enhance our lives and prepare us for our journey to heaven? What is your purpose here on Earth?

Time and Space

Time and space are our gifts from above.
It is the belief in both that creates our love.
In this method of intervals, we are able to correct our ways.
Time is so that we can start a new cycle every day.
Without time on Earth, we would never have the four seasons.
We would not expand our knowledge or act with reason.
The next thought would be "Why the existence of space?"
Without space, we never would move on to a new place.
Time and space are really one and the same.
To move in space, time is the factor on this plane.
Without space, a view of the mountains would not be,
For space creates our perception of everything we see.

Time Flies

We live our life and it is controlled by time.
Never a moment is it not on our mind.
Wherever we go, we always have this reminder.
Time is important, but we are like a horse with blinders.
We wear it, hand it, and place it on our desk.
Tick tock, tick tock—the sound has never a moment to rest.
Tick tock, tick tock as time moves from start to finish.
We live through these intervals where time is diminished,
So how can we cope with this ruler of time?
Just sit back and accept this law, for all will be fine.
Originally published in *Spiritual Path to Wisdom*, 2015.

Train

Evolution on the Train

From start to finish, all of us ride on the same "train." As some of us gain knowledge and wisdom we exit the train and rise to Heaven.

This train can be considered evolution from start to finish. When you get on the train, you might be an insect, and then you evolve. You die and come back as a butterfly and get back on the train and evolve and evolve until one time you climb aboard as a present-day man. When this man has finished his evolution, then he will be at the end of his train ride and will rise to the heavenly Father above.

It is the job of those that are ahead in wisdom and knowledge to aid others on the train to grow, mature, and evolve toward perfection.

When the train with the people of perfection is empty because they have all risen to the heavenly Father, then it goes back and picks up another load of those who have more evolution to go through.

This is the cycle of life, or evolution!

The Train

Boarding the train is such an easy feat.
Find a place as you are led to your seat.
Prepare for your ride, for evolution is about to begin.
This is your journey, for many treasures lie within.
Evolution, you will find, is a long and complex affair.
You will experience many life forms with a new flair.
This will be an adventure—a very pleasant ride
Moving through billions of years with Spirit at your side.
You may even start your trip as a lower life form.
You will evolve and continue onward to transform.
Eventually as a final step, a human you will become.
Your journey is almost over, as all stages you have done.
There is never a feeling to hurry to rush evolution to its end.
The heavenly Father has guided your path, and for you he will send.

Where Are You Going?

How many times have you said to yourself, "What is in store for me after this life here on Earth?" Over the years, we have all heard stories of people who have had near-death experiences in which they arrived in a beautiful field of flowers and saw friends and families in the distance. But then all the people turned their backs and walked away, and the person returned back to Earth to continue among the living.

I remember my mother-in-law being in the hospital and very ill. She told me an experience she'd had in which she was up near the ceiling, looking down at all the doctors and nurses surrounding her bed. She said it was truly an out-of-body experience. She told me she then she dropped down and returned to her physical body.

The Bible tells many stories of people being raised from the death to continue on with life. There are many people who believe that after death you will either go to heaven and stand before God at the pearly gates or perhaps go to purgatory and appear before Lucifer, the fallen angel.

Before there even was a planet Earth, God was preparing a place for his children to live. In six days, he completed this work, and in time he created man and woman. Therefore, all children born on this planet are a result of God's divine plan. He knew each and every one of us before we were even conceived.

As God is our creator, he does have a plan set for each and every one of us. But God tests us all the time, and sometimes we may win and sometimes we may lose. Let's look at the disciple Paul and see how he transformed his life. Born as a Jew, Paul was originally called Saul of Tarsus, and he was a persecutor of all the Christians. He believed it was his responsibility to persecute those found worshipping the Lord

God and being followers of Jesus Christ. This was not the path the true God had set out for his child, Paul. As a devoted Jew, Paul knew the Word of God, and in time he was converted by the Word of God to follow Jesus Christ. When appearing before God in heaven, he surely entered the pearly gates.

The book of Job tells of the faithfulness and trust of one man for his God. Satan made a pact with God that he could turn this man away from God and claim him as his own. Thus, Job was tested over and over again, but never once did he give up his faith in the Lord. I guess we know that when he appeared before the Lord, he, too, passed through the pearly gates.

What about Adam and Eve, as they did not pass the test the Lord God gave them? They disobeyed and lost faith in God and were ashamed. What do you think happened to them when they appeared before God at the time of reckoning? They are the children of the Lord God, and I cannot believe he would send them to live for eternity in the fiery pit of hell.

King David could be said to be both good and bad. Yes, he took down Goliath by trusting in the Lord, but then he sinned with Bathsheba, and even worse, he had her husband killed so he could marry her. Yet his man wrote some of the most beautiful psalms of love and trust. David was not a man of peace, but he was greatly loved by the people. In what direction did David go when he died?

Let's look at the life of Judas Iscariot, who was one of the twelve disciples and a close friend to Jesus. Judas was God's child, and God had a plan for him before he was even born. In order for Christ Jesus to be raised from the dead, he had to be betrayed and convicted. Someone had to be the bad guy and betray Jesus Christ, and this role was given to Judas. This weighted heavily on Judas's heart, and in the end, he killed himself because of his shame; but this is the role God had planned for him. He carried out this important plan the Lord God had for him; he obeyed the role set before him. So when Judas died, who sat in judgment of him?

If we look into the beliefs of many of the American Indians, we find they thought of death as a "transition," like a journey from one world to the next. Some of them believe that at death the soul goes on its own journey and joins up with the souls of other ancestors. Others believe that life and death are part of one big cycle that many today call reincarnation. In this concept, they believe that the elders can remember the past because they have already lived it. This is why the Indians would leave their older people who were ill and weak on the side of the path to be killed by wild animals or exposure. Only their physical bodies would die, but their souls would be lifted up and soar. So according to this belief, at death there is no heaven or hell; there is an ongoing cycle of rebirth.

If one looks into the belief of Buddhism, one finds that Buddhists believe in reincarnation. There are various stages one must go through in this process. Consider it a learning curve along each stage of which one hopefully learns new lessons and advances to the next stage. There are six karmic realms of rebirth: heavenly beings, demigods, humans, animals, ghosts, and residents of hell. So, to a student of Buddhism, one is constantly being reborn so one can advance oneself to the final step, which is heavenly.

I have always so enjoyed the story of the "Evolution on the Train." There have been many different versions of this theme, but I like the one Ned and I did in 2014.

So the big question is, Where are you going? Mother once said to me as she was nearing the end of her time here on Earth, "I cannot believe, with all the knowledge I have gained over the years, that death will be the end of it." I agree with her that God has a plan for us and that it is not finished in the time we have allotted on this planet earth. Like the Indians, I feel that my ancestors are near and helping to guide me on this pathway. Like Buddhists, I feel that we are reborn and will keep coming back until we reach that higher plateau and finally rise to heaven to be with our heavenly Father and all our ancestors.

Airplane Ride

I visualized a 747 in flight. From stem to stern, it had a passenger in every other seat—each from a different walk of life. I was sitting in the last rear seat. It came to me that all these people were me from past reincarnations.

One by one, I sat next to each entity and discussed its life. As I completed my talk with each one, it blended into my existing self. I wove each personality and trait into my own being—both good and bad, right and wrong. I did not fight these beings but rather blended them with my own vibration.

You see now why we feel so many feelings in every moment, for we are not one entity but many entities rolled into one. Accept this as truth. Weave this vibration into one of a higher nature. When you feel a loose thread, bring it back to the fold.

When I got to the last seat, I had my house in order and for the first time knew I was many. To perform self-simulation is to blend the many into one and know oneself. As this point I entered the cockpit to meet the captain and take control of my own life.

Past Life's Revelation

Read my journal writing entitled "Airplane Ride," which was written some thirty years ago. This is why it is so important for us to keep journals where we can write down our thoughts and feelings. As we find our own words and perceptions, we all evolve in wisdom. Because of this airplane revelation, I now have a much deeper spiritual grasp of its meaning. The empty seats were our invisible spirit guides.

Nothing in our path ever goes unwritten in our DNA. It is all recorded. Trillions and trillions of facts never ever seen, heard, or spoken are there. These are all part of what we are today. We have only one mind, yet it records two perceptions of our lifetimes in our objective, or conscious, mind and also in the subconscious inner mind.

The role of the brain is for the present lifetime only. It has no power to control the body. It is only to take orders from our universal mind. Our lifeline from our Holy Spirit, is that buzzing in our ear that we all need to stop and listen to.

Words

Jesus said: "Listen and understand. What goes into a man's mouth does not make him unclean, but what comes out of his mouth, that is what makes him unclean."

—Matthew 15:10 (NIV)

Open Your Mind

What always amazes me is that humans view the animal kingdom as less intelligent than themselves. Take a young dog, for example. It takes months to train a young dog, but it walks almost immediately. Yet a human baby may take a year to learn to walk.

Because we are not able to understand how they talk and communicate with one another, do we think less of the animal kingdom? They don't chatter like humans. They, like us, have brains and hearts, and blood flows through their systems as it does through ours. So why is there the idea that we are smarter?

Here is an example.

A bald eagle with a wingspan of five feet goes from a dead stop on the ground to the air just by flapping its wings. The mother flying in and out of its nest puts in the young ones' minds that they, too, can fly. Tell me, how does a spider know how to weave a perfect web? How is it that an ant can carry 100 times its own weight or a flea jump thirteen feet?

My goal in life at seventy-seven years of age is to awaken everyone's mind to see the true reality around us and behold the wonders of other creatures that are all here in service to us. I ask you to look and listen to the miracles around you. Creation, intelligent design and free will—it is all the same to me.

Open Your Mind

I just can't help the powerful need to write,
For I know that words have such might.
With proper arrangement, words have such power.
You can get these feelings hour after hour.
See also the wildlife so fancy and free.
It lifts our spirits, for once they were you and me
A view from the mountaintop, all covered with snow,
Makes us wonder, "Is this beauty all for show?"
This world is so orderly, with various perfections.
We wonder at times why we fall into rejections.
Our problem is that we lose sight of our goal,
For we are here to listen, to enlighten, as it does unfold.

The Word Was God

In the Bible, the Word of God is referred to over and over again.

> In the beginning was the Word, and the Word was with God, and the Word was God. (John 1:1 KJV)

> For this cause also thank we God without ceasing, because, when ye received the word of God which ye heard of us, ye received *it* not *as* the word of men, but as it is in truth, the word of God, which effectually worketh also in you that believe. (1 Thessalonians 2:13 KJV)

> For the word of God is living and active. Sharper than any double-edged sword, it penetrates even to dividing soul and spirit, joints and marrow; it judges the thoughts and attitudes of the heart. (Hebrews 4:12 NIV)

There are many people in this world that have hardened hearts and refuse to hear the Word of God. God made men perfect, in his image and likeness. To each of us he gave a special gift, a talent, an inquisitive mind, and the power of free will. As stated in Colossians 1:16–17 (KJV), "For by him were all things created, that are in heaven, and that are in earth, visible and invisible, whether *they be* thrones, or dominions, or principalities, or powers: all things were created by him, and for him." This is the Lord God using mankind to invent and create new things. These inventions that the Bible speaks of are man's use of the power of his Word to develop new ideas and create many advanced things.

Mankind is not smart enough to come up with all the inventions on his own. He hears the Word of God and develops his theory from there. This is how the wheel, the auto, the airplane, and the exploration of outer space have occurred—by the Word from God conveyed to his children.

Words

Have you ever thought about what your mind conjures up for just the use of one simple word?

Whether you use just one word or a string of words put together, you can end up with so many different meanings and feelings. Take the word "love," for example. What does this bring to mind—your family, a pet, a favorite food, a pillow? On and on your thoughts run. But now the words, "I Love You," and you come up with a completely different context—a feeling of being cherished, being special, being accepted, and belonging. You are now experiencing an emotion, whereas the single word makes you think of material things you love.

There is a tremendous power in the written or spoken word. Just take writing a résumé, an important speech, a letter, or a note to a child. What is written on the paper and read by others is a lifelong document. The words can be harsh or tender, positive or negative, sparkling or dull, truthful or dishonest. The list continues to grow.

How many times have you heard these phrases?

1. She has kept her word.
2. Actions speak louder than words.
3. He put in a good word for me.
4. In a word, the situation is serious.
5. He is a person of few words.
6. She is a woman of her word.
7. Here is a word to the wise.

In times of great stress, we turn to prayer or have a silent conversation with God. There is no need to speak out loud, but in silence we say the words that are in our hearts to obtain healing and release. God knows our thoughts before we even form the words. Where would any of us be without being able to use various words to communicate what we are feeling?

You have heard people say, "Those are fighting words," and then get into a brawl or fistfight. So, words can also spark anger, fear, abuse, and so many negative emotions. So again, be careful that the words you speak do not cause anger in other people.

If it were not for the written word, none of us would know what had transpired in history. There would be no books on Napoleon Bonaparte, Caesar Augustus, Queen Victoria, Jesus Christ, the US Constitution, or anything else right up to our current time. Even today, how many of us keep a journal or diary to record, in written words, our feelings from day to day?

Throughout our daily lives, it is important to remember how the words we use can affect other people for an entire day. A happy "Hello, how are you?" is so much stronger than a complaint or a scowl or even indifference as you pass someone on the street or in the office. Happy people are contagious, so use only happy, kind words.

It is interesting that as part of the laws of the universe there is the power of opposites. The same holds true for words: "love" vs. "hate," "hot vs. cold," "happy vs. sad," "kind vs. cruel," and so on. For so many words, there are opposites.

The written word can take us to faraway places and new adventures while sitting in our own easy chair. Sit down with a good book and learn all about Eleanor Roosevelt, Billy Graham, and so many others. Perhaps you enjoy living in the science fiction environment, or maybe you prefer a good murder mystery or a beautiful love story. Words can take us to places in our imagination we never dreamed of.

The spoken word in church can give us a feeling of serenity. Debates can spark our interest and help us learn more about various subjects. Political discussions can help us to decide whom to vote for. In essence, the Word can describe who you are, what you are, and what you will become.

In closing I would like to advise you to listen to that small voice in your head, watch what words come out of your mouth, and be aware of what you write down in print. "In the beginning was the Word, and the Word was with God, and the Word was God" (John 1:1 NIV).

The Art of Talking

There is a perfect example of miscommunication,
For our words may be misjudged by your interpretation.
With the use of words, many have different meanings,
And some may take them to be very demeaning.
Because our perception is due to our past history,
The way we talk may end up being a mystery.
Yet if we talk to each other in a neutral way,
We express ourselves so each understands what we say.

The Mouth Is the Voice

The mouth is a mighty tool we all possess.
How we use it determines our personality at best.
Take a singer with the beautiful sounds they convey,
Or the preacher with a sermon that leads us to pray.
The words that come out can be loving and gentle,
But the words can be harsh and foul, not at all subtle.
Words can be hurtful, which is hard to take back.
Unkind words just show there is something we lack.
Words of prayer can have such a healing effect.
Think with your heart, and what comes out will be perfect.
Use your voice for good and to praise our father above.
Words from the heart will resound like the wings of love.

When It Is Gone, It Is Gone

Words that fly out of our mouths are forever gone.
Time is gone with each sunset and early dawn.
How about that opportunity you let pass by?
Gone forever is that chance to reach for the sky.
What are we letting slip through our fingers each day?
Love and hope—these emotions can come into play.
Be sure what is important to you isn't gone forever.
Our Creator is available to help us work this together.
Our silent prayers will be answered one by one.
With God at our side we will surely get this job done.

Words and Phrases

An Eye for an Eye

Some people feel that an eye for an eye or the "law" of retaliation is the principle that a person who has injured another person is penalized to a similar degree. The phrase "an eye for an eye" is mentioned in several chapters of the Old Testament of the Bible (Exodus, Leviticus, and Deuteronomy), but it was never intended to mean that physical damage should be done to another person. It was never God's intent to harm any of his children. We are made in his image and likeness, so why would he want us to maim a person he created, which is a perfect magnification of him? It is a phrase made to make us think. Our free will determines how we will interpret it.

Jesus taught that we are not to seek revenge for a wrongdoing; instead we are to go above and beyond what is asked of us. As stated in Matthew 5:39 (NIV), "But I tell you, Do not resist an evil person. If someone strikes you on the right cheek, turn to him the other cheek also."

We, as believers and children of God, must learn to forgive and love everyone. Paul wrote, "Do not repay anyone evil for evil. Be careful to do what is right in the eyes of everyone" (Romans 12:17 NIV).

Ask and You Shall Receive

In the Sermon on the Mount, Jesus stated, "Ask and it will be given to you; seek and you will find; knock and the door will be opened to you. For everyone who asks receives; he who seeks finds; and to him who knocks, the door will be opened" (Matthew 7:7–8 NIV). Do you think that Jesus used this phrase so you would ask to find a one-hundred-dollar bill on the ground, or perhaps so you would ask for the shiny new red sports car at the dealership that you so desperately want? Asking the Lord God for material possessions on this planet is not what Jesus was speaking about.

When in communication with the Lord God, Jesus, or our Holy Spirit, we can ask for freedom from a disease, freedom from despair, and freedom from want. If we pray fervently and sincerely, a door may be opened to us. It may not be the answer we were praying for, but it will be the path God has set out for us. The door will open to other prospects, and we will receive the blessing of the Lord.

Remember that God does answer every prayer request, but he will do so in his time, not in ours. God knows the right time and the right place to answer our prayers. God may put a spin on our prayer request, and his answer will be so much more powerful than our original request. Be patient and you will receive!

Become Like Little Children

"I tell you the truth, unless you change and become like little children, you will never enter the kingdom of heaven" (Matthew 18:3 NIV). In Biblical times, little children had no status; they were unimportant and not even members of society. So often when Jesus did his preaching, it was to these same status-less members of society. These are the ones Jesus wanted to save so they would have a place in the kingdom of heaven.

Little children are born into this life as innocent beings, free of sin and with trusting hearts. These are the qualities that Jesus identifies as necessary for entrance to the kingdom. These little children are dependent on their parents for all their daily needs, including food, shelter, security, and a sense of belonging.

To become like little children is to be trusting and have faith in the Father. As adults, we should have this same trust and faith in our heavenly Father. Through daily worship, meditation, and prayer, we also should be dependent on our Father for our daily needs. "I tell you the truth, anyone who will not receive the kingdom of God like a little child will never enter it" (Luke 18:17 NIV).

Eye of a Needle

"But Jesus said again, 'Children, how hard is it to enter the kingdom of God! It is easier for a camel to go through the eye of a needle than for a rich man to enter the kingdom of God'" (Mark 10:24–25 NIV).

Does this statement mean that anyone who is rich will not be able to enter the kingdom of heaven? Do you think Jesus wanted this statement to be taken literally? This is similar to the many parables that are recorded in the Bible, and there is a lesson to be learned in it.

We know that in a camel, which is large, going through the eye of a needle, which is very small, the contrast in size emphasizes the unimportance of material wealth and possessions. It also shows that it would be easier to go through the eye of a needle than to give away all your money and to live like Jesus. The task of going through the eye of the needle proves to be a futile act.

In this statement, Jesus is emphasizing that we are not to place such importance in our material wealth. Your ability to enter the kingdom of heaven, whether you are rich or poor, depends on your spiritual character. Keep the Ten Commandments, live by the Golden Rule, and pray without ceasing. Remember as Jesus said "…but with God all things are possible." (Matthew 19: 26 (KJV)

For the love of money is a root of all kinds of evils

"For the love of money is a root of all kinds of evils. Some people, eager for money, have wandered from the faith and pierced themselves with many griefs" (1 Timothy 6:10 NIV).

The Bible often refers to the treasures in heaven. This passage from the Bible sums it up quite eloquently: "Do not store up for yourselves treasures on earth, where moth and rust destroy, and where thieves break in and steal. But store up for yourselves treasures in heaven, where moth and rust do not destroy, and where thieves do not break in and steal. For where your treasure is, there your heart will be also" (Matthew 6:19–22 NIV).

How many times have you heard the phrases "golden age," "golden parachute," and "golden touch"? What do these make you think of? Unfortunately, many of us in the twenty-first century are overly concerned with material possessions: a new car, a boat, a plane, a house, a closet full of clothes, and on and on this list goes.

As children, we are brought into this world with nothing—not even clothes for our backs. We all know that is exactly the same way we will leave this earthly planet: with nothing—not even the clothes on our backs. But, during our time on this planet, so often we try so hard to accumulate wealth and costly possessions. Unfortunately, these are material possessions. But what of those spiritual possessions that are so important for us in our spiritual growth?

The Bible states that no one can serve two masters. Who is your master? As children of faith, it is our job to take care of the needy, feed the hungry, clothe the poor, and lift up the fallen in spirit. Do not let wealth become your master; instead give your heart and soul to others to make their lives fuller.

Our true example of someone who did all these things for the poor, the sick, and the sinner is our Lord Jesus Christ. We never hear of Jesus carrying a suitcase around with fancy clothes and extra shoes. No, he slept on the ground or in the home of the tax collector. Take him as an example of how to be humble and loving to all people. Watch out for God's people, and God will surely watch out for you.

"One man gives freely, yet gains even more; another withholds unduly, but comes to poverty. A generous man will prosper; he who refreshes others will himself be refreshed" (Proverbs 11:24–25 NVI).

He Who Is Without Sin, Cast the First Stone

"If any one of you is without sin, let him be the first to throw a stone at her" (John 8:7 NVI). This is a very powerful message that Jesus said to the teachers of the law and the Pharisees when they wanted Jesus to uphold the law of Moses by permitting them to stone a woman who had been caught in adultery. Yet not one stone was cast at this woman, and the reason is simple: not one person in that crowd, be he or she a teacher or a religious leader, was "without sin."

In our own private lives, it is so important that we do not judge others, for that is not our job. The Lord God is the only one in a position to judge his children. Only Jesus was made perfect and without sin, but he had to die for us on the cross so our sins were forgiven.

There are many reasons why we may feel we have the right to judge our fellow men or be critical of their lifestyle. Perhaps our thinking is not like theirs, or we might feel they are unkind to others; perhaps they do not keep the Ten Commandments. We never have the right to judge others; we can pray for them, and we can show them the way by example, but we may not cast that first stone.

We have all heard the old proverb, "Those who live in glass houses should not throw stones." A good interpretation of this is that one should not criticize others for having the same faults as oneself. In other words, we have all committed sins, even if only through a verbal comment, a secret wish, or an action. Therefore, it is not proper for us to point out the sins another has committed when we have also sinned.

The Golden Rule

From early childhood, we have been taught the Golden Rule: "Do unto others as you would have them do unto you." What a wonderful statement to be reinforced to each child and adult. On the playground, you would not say unkind words to a friend, as you would not want your friend to do the same to you. As an adult on the job, you would not want to be known as a backstabber in order to get ahead in business, because you would not want someone to do that to you.

Jesus told his disciples and others, "So in everything, do unto others what you would have them do to you, for this sums up the Law and the Prophets" (Matthew 7:12 NIV). Even Confucius, who lived many years before Christ, stated, "Do not do to others what you would not want others to do to you." It is Amazing that these two men had the same thought though they lived so many years apart. Does this not reinforce that God has a plan for his children regardless of the time frame?

Keep in mind that Jesus's words were positive reinforcement: "Do unto others" rather than the negative "Do not do." Jesus also stated, "Love your neighbor as yourself." (Mark 12: 31 NIV) This being the case, you would never want to harm your neighbor; you would want to treat your neighbor as you also treat yourself—with love, respect, and kindness.

The Meek Shall Inherit the Earth

"Blessed are the meek, for they will inherit the earth" (Matthew 5:5 NIV).

It can be stated that to be meek is to be humble, have full trust in God, and be a gentle soul. The meek are often shy and timid, but with a patient and gentle attitude toward all others. These are the followers God has chosen to lead his people and find the kingdom of heaven.

If you think of the various men who have experienced the Word of God, you will find them to be of the meek personality. Moses was a gentle soul who trusted in the Lord God; Job trusted in the Lord through all his hardships. Daniel, Noah and so many others could also be described as meek.

Meekness is not a negative trait but one of willingness to hear the Word of God and accept it. We are to trust that God is in control of our lives and to obey in order to inherit the riches of heaven.

What is in the earth that shall be inherited? Is it the soil, the sea, and all plant life here on planet Earth, or is it a more spiritual place? Jesus stated in the Sermon on the Mount, "Your kingdom come, your will be done on earth, as it is in heaven" (Matthew 6:10 NIV). Might it be that "earth" is not a physical mass but refers to inheritance of the land, or earth, by whatever name you call it, in the kingdom of heaven? "But the meek will inherit the land and enjoy great peace" (Psalm 37:11 NIV).

You Are the Salt of the Earth

Have you ever heard someone state, "He is the salt of the earth"? What exactly does that phrase mean? One needs to understand the meaning and properties of salt to get a better understanding of this phrase.

In biblical times, salt was a rare and expensive commodity. It was prized for keeping food products from spoiling; it was used as an antiseptic or cleaning agent. Hebrew women would rub their newborn babies with salt as a cleansing procedure. Salt cannot make something good; it can only keep something from becoming bad.

Jesus placed high expectations on his followers and on what he required of them. He stated, "You are the salt of the earth" (Matthew 5:13 NIV). Salt was something rare in that time—something of great value to be prized and to be protected. Thus, Jesus knew that his disciples and followers were that same rare commodity.

We should cleanse, season, and purify our surroundings by our attitudes and actions toward all those around us. Jesus tells us that when we show kindness to those who are hurting, comfort to those who are lost, and encouragement to those in need, we are sprinkling the seasoning of salt to all those around us. When salt maintains its integrity to preserve, the effects are long-lasting and permanent.

We are to be a seasoning agent in this world. We will see the salt effect in the changed lives, values, meaning, and purpose in God's people. So, if a man is called "the salt of the earth," he is someone with integrity, showing kindness to all regardless of their race, color, or gender. He is one of great value to be prized among men.

Vengeance Is Mine

How many times are we faced with a problem where someone has done an unkindness against us and we want to retaliate or get even? It causes one's temper to rise, makes one's blood boil, and moves one to take action in order to correct what he or she feels has been an injustice to them.

But wait and think this through. The Bible says, "Do not take revenge, my friends, but leave room for God's wrath, for it is written: It is mine to avenge; I will repay, says the Lord … Do not say, 'I'll pay you back for this wrong!' Wait for the LORD, and he will deliver you" (Romans 12:19; Proverbs 20:22 NIV). It is the wise man who turns the other cheek and lets our Lord God handle the situation. It may not happen this week or this year, but our Lord God will avenge the wrong done unto you.

Trying to get even and hurt the other person does more harm to you than to the other individual. After avenging the wrong, do you really feel better? Have you expressed the unkind and evil side of yourself? Have you then been the one who has committed a sin and must try to obtain forgiveness?

Move on, forgive that person, erase the event from your mind, and move forward.

Notes and Comments

Notes and Comments

Printed in the United States
By Bookmasters